"For God so loved the world that he gave his only begotten Son, in order that whoever believes in him will not be destroyed but have eternal life."

JOHN 3:16

JOHN 3:16

For God So Loved the World

EDWARD D. ANDREWS

JOHN 3:16

For God So Loved the World

Edward D. Andrews

Christian Publishing House

Cambridge, Ohio

CHRISTIAN
PUBLISHING
HOUSE

FOUNDED 2005

Unless otherwise stated, Scripture quotations are from Updated American Standard Version (UASV) Copyright © 2022 by Christian Publishing House

JOHN 3:16: For God So Loved the World by Edward D. Andrews

ISBN-10: 1945757566

ISBN-13: 978-1945757563

Table of Contents

Book Description

In "JOHN 3:16: For God So Loved the World," the author embarks on a profound exploration of one of the most iconic verses in the Christian Scriptures. A verse that encapsulates the essence of God's incredible love for humanity and the salvation He offers through His son, Jesus Christ.

Starting with a thought-provoking introduction on the unparalleled gift of God's only-begotten Son, the book systematically delves into each segment of John 3:16. Each chapter brings to life the depth and breadth of the love, sacrifice, trust, and eternal hope encapsulated in this singular verse. The author also takes a refreshing turn by drawing out practical applications, teaching readers how they can emulate divine love in their daily lives and how they can act in harmony with Jesus' prayers.

Moreover, "JOHN 3:16: For God So Loved the World" ventures into discerning the requirements of a Godly life, exploring themes of love, unity, and the pathway to eternal happiness. The latter chapters form a synthesis of theology and practice, urging readers to not just believe, but to internalize and act upon their faith.

In this carefully curated exploration of John 3:16, the readers are offered a transformative journey from understanding God's immense love to realizing their role in reflecting that love to the world. Complete with a bibliography for those keen on further study, this book is an essential read for anyone seeking a deeper, more enriched faith journey.

Preface

John 3:16 is more than just a verse that many of us learned in Sunday school or noticed on a banner in a sports stadium. It is the heart of the Gospel message, a profound statement of hope, love, and the promise of eternal life. In a world that often seems filled with chaos, uncertainty, and despair, the words "For God so loved the world" offer a beacon of light.

In the following pages, we don't just dissect this beloved Scripture line by line. Instead, we embark on a spiritual journey, delving deep into the essence of God's love and the salvation story. This exploration is not just about understanding the historical and theological context of the verse but about making it a living reality in our daily lives.

My goal in writing this book was not only to provide a comprehensive understanding of John 3:16 but also to encourage every reader to reflect upon their personal relationship with God. How have we experienced His love? How do we respond to the incredible gift of His son, Jesus Christ? And how can we live our lives in a way that reflects our gratitude and commitment to Him?

As we journey through each chapter, my hope is that you find renewed inspiration, deeper faith, and a more intimate connection with our Creator. May the insights within these pages not just inform but transform, leading each one of us closer to the heart of God and the eternal life He promises.

Edward D. Andrews

Author of 220+ books and Chief Translator of the Updated American Standard Version

INTRODUCTION
For God Gave His Only Begotten Son

John 3:16 Updated American Standard Version (UASV)

16 For God so loved the world that he gave his **only-begotten Son**, in order that everyone trusting in him will not be destroyed but have eternal life.

The Nuances of "Only Begotten Son" in John 3:16: A Greek Perspective

The phrase "only begotten Son" translates the Greek term "μονογενὴς υἱός" (monogenēs huios) as it appears in John 3:16 in the Greek New Testament. The term "μονογενὴς" (monogenēs) has been the subject of extensive debate among scholars and translators. This term is a compound of "μόνος" (monos), meaning "only," and a second element that is often linked to "γένος" (genos), meaning "kind" or "type," or to the verb "γίνομαι" (ginomai), meaning "to become" or "to be born." The focus here will be on examining why "only begotten Son" remains the preferred translation.

Linguistic Precision

The term "μονογενὴς" (monogenēs) carries more weight than merely being "only" or "unique." It implies a unique relationship that has no parallel, and it suggests an origin—the "begetting" aspect. This aspect is lost when translations opt for "his only Son" or "one and only Son."

Historical Theological Context

The phrase "only begotten" has historical theological significance rooted in the early Christian understanding of the relationship between the Father and the Son. During the Arian controversy of the 4th century, for instance, the nature of this relationship was hotly debated. The term "only begotten" was used to refute the Arian claim that the Son was a created being, emphasizing instead that the Son was "begotten, not made," in the words of the Nicene Creed. Therefore, using the term "only begotten" aligns with historical, orthodox Christian theology.

Textual Tradition

In the realm of textual criticism, it's worth noting that the term "μονογενὴς υἱός" (monogenēs huios) appears consistently in the most reliable Greek manuscripts of the New Testament. Therefore, from a textual standpoint, there's a strong argument to be made for retaining the original phraseology in translation.

Comparative Linguistic Analysis

It is also informative to look at other instances where the term "μονογενὴς" (monogenēs) appears in the New

Testament. For example, Hebrews 11:17 refers to Isaac as Abraham's "only begotten" son. While Abraham had other sons, Isaac was the only son "begotten" through Sarah, fulfilling God's promise in a unique way. This highlights the unique relationship and specific circumstances that the term "only begotten" encompasses.

Interpretive Consistency

One might argue that adopting a more generalized translation like "only" or "one and only" could open the door to unwarranted theological extrapolations. For instance, using just "only" could imply that there are other "sons" in a different sense. The term "only begotten" specifies the unique Father-Son relationship that exists between God and Jesus, thereby maintaining theological clarity.

Conclusion

The term "only begotten Son" serves not merely as a translational choice but as a doctrinal statement rooted in the very words of Scripture. It is an integral part of Christian heritage, reflecting the unique, uncreated nature of the Son and His special relationship with the Father. Hence, from a standpoint that values linguistic precision, historical theology, textual tradition, comparative linguistic analysis, and interpretive consistency, "only begotten Son" remains the preferred choice for translating "μονογενὴς υἱός" in John 3:16.

Decoding the Term "Only-Begotten Son" in Biblical Greek

The Complexities of the Greek Word "Monogenes"

The Greek term "monogenes" is traditionally translated as "only-begotten," and it carries hefty theological weight. It emphasizes that Jesus, the divine Son of God, was not created by the Father but was "eternally generated" by Him. The two have existed together forever, indicating a unique relationship between them.

The Debate on "Genos" vs. "Gennetos"

Scholars who specialize in Greek point out that "monogenes" is actually built on the Greek word "genos," not "gennetos," which directly translates to "begotten." Because of this, some argue that the term should mean "unique" or "one of a kind" rather than "only-begotten." However, this isn't the complete picture.

Dictionary Definitions and Family Connections

In a comprehensive Greek lexicon by Liddell, Scott, Jones, and McKenzie, "monogenes" is defined as "the only member of a kin or kind." This offers us some flexibility in translation. For example, "monogenes" could imply the only natural-born child in a family, differentiating from adopted children. The term "monogennetos" might seem more precise for this situation, but that word doesn't actually exist in ancient Greek. So, "monogenes" gets the job done.

Language Barriers and Theological Considerations

A major hurdle we face is that modern English lacks an ideal term to express this concept. While some may argue that "only-begotten" sounds outdated, using alternatives like "natural" or "biological" creates problems when trying to describe the supernatural origin of Jesus.

Theological Concerns with Alternative Terms

Let's say Jesus is just the "only" or "one and only" Son of God. That raises the question: What about Christians, who are also considered children of God (Hebrews 2:11)? We could call Jesus "unique," but that's a bland term that lacks theological depth.

The Puzzle of John 1:18

Another dilemma occurs in John 1:18, where the term "monogenes" is used to describe God. If we use "one and only," we're left with a confusing statement about God's uniqueness, which doesn't clearly distinguish between the Father and the Son. However, "only-begotten" clarifies that the text refers to Jesus, endorsing His divinity.

John 1:18 Updated American Standard Version (UASV)

[18] No one has seen God at any time; the only begotten God* who is in the bosom of the Father, that one has made him fully known.

* The original words were μονογενὴς θεός or ο μονογενης θεος "only-begotten God" or "the only-begotten God" (P[66] P[75] א B C* L 33 syr[hmp] 33 cop[bo]) A variant reading is ο μονογενης υιος "the only begotten Son" A C[3] (W[s]) Θ Ψ f[1,] Maj syr[c]).

The Linguistic Challenge

The term "only-begotten" might seem old-fashioned or challenging, but it serves a critical function. It maintains the theological significance carried by the original Greek word. The term may not have an exact counterpart in modern English, but its essence cannot be replaced by lesser alternatives like "only" or "unique."

Conclusion: The Ongoing Importance of "Only-Begotten"

In summary, while "only-begotten" might sound archaic, it captures a vital theological truth that other terms fail to convey. The challenge lies in the limitations of earthly language to describe heavenly concepts. Until we find a more fitting term, "only-begotten" remains invaluable for preserving this essential Christian belief.

Exegetical Commentary on John 3:16

Contextual Background

John 3:16 is one of the most famous verses in the New Testament, set in the context of Jesus' dialogue with Nicodemus, a Pharisee and member of the Sanhedrin. This interaction focuses on the essentiality of being "born again" to see the Kingdom of God. The verse itself encapsulates the Gospel message and serves as a cornerstone for Christian soteriology.

Phrase-by-Phrase Analysis

"For God so loved the world"

The Greek phrase here is "Οὕτως γὰρ ἠγάπησεν ὁ Θεὸς τὸν κόσμον." The word "ἠγάπησεν" (agapēsen) signifies a love that is unconditional, self-sacrificing, and deliberate. This kind of love is not just emotional but volitional, stemming from God's nature. The term "κόσμον" (kosmon) refers to the world in its entirety, indicating that God's redemptive plan extends beyond Israel to include all of humanity.

"that he gave his only begotten Son"

The Greek reads "ὥστε τὸν Υἱὸν αὐτοῦ τὸν μονογενῆ ἔδωκεν." The word "μονογενῆ" (monogenē) is critical here. As discussed earlier, this term signifies "only-begotten," implying a unique and unparalleled relationship between the Father and the Son. It's a term that carries heavy theological weight, stressing the Son's eternal generation and uniqueness.

"in order that whoever believes in him"

The phrase "ἵνα πᾶς ὁ πιστεύων εἰς αὐτὸν" pinpoints the condition for redemption: faith. The word "πιστεύων" (pisteuōn) means more than intellectual assent; it involves entrusting oneself entirely to Jesus. The preposition "εἰς" (eis) denotes a forward motion, a leaning into, which amplifies the notion that true belief is an active, relational trust.

"will not be destroyed but have eternal life"

Finally, "μὴ ἀπόληται ἀλλ᾽ ἔχῃ ζωὴν αἰώνιον" spells out the outcome of such faith. The term "ἀπόληται" (apolētai) means to be destroyed or to perish, presenting a dire contrast to "ζωὴν αἰώνιον" (zōēn aiōnion), or eternal life. The term "αἰώνιον" (aiōnion) is not just everlasting life in terms of length but also a qualitative change—life in a relationship with God that starts now and continues eternally.

Theological Implications

John 3:16 encapsulates the essence of the Gospel: God's redemptive love through the unique Son, the condition of faith, and the promise of eternal life. The term "only-begotten" is of great importance because it emphasizes the distinct role of Jesus as the Son who is of the same essence as the Father, marking Him as the only viable pathway to eternal life.

CHAPTER 1 For God So Loved the World

John 3:16 Updated American Standard Version (UASV)

[16] **For God so loved the world** that he gave his only-begotten Son, in order that everyone trusting in him will not be destroyed but have eternal life.

Appreciating the Sacrifice

There is no culture in the history where its people do not show their love and appreciate for a friend who has died. If we think of a military hero that has come home from fighting for the freedom of his country, the love and appreciation are even stronger because of the sacrifice he[1] made. Every person who has accepted Jesus Christ since the first-century Christian era has an even greater reason to show their love and appreciation, as they now have the hope of eternal life.—2 Corinthians 5:14; 1 John 2:2.

Appreciating the Father's Sacrifice

Returning to the soldier that has just sacrificed his life for the freedom of his country, we also have a tremendous

---

[1] We are using the masculine pronoun here because Jesus was a man. However, we are well aware of the sacrifices that many women have given for their country.

love and appreciation for the father[2] of the fallen soldier. The sacrifice of his son for our freedom is very moving and motivating. The Father of the Son had to watch as Jesus Christ sacrificed himself as a ransom for redeemable humankind. Jesus said of his Father, reminding us "For God so loved the world that he gave his only-begotten Son …"

Appreciating the Son's Sacrifice

When a fallen soldier comes home from war, thousands and sometimes tens of thousands come to his funeral to express their love and appreciation for his sacrifice in behalf of our country. Jesus tells us, "the Son of Man came … to give his soul as a ransom for many." Jesus also tells us that he was willing to do the will of the Father, to offer himself in our behalf. ", "Truly, truly, I say to you, the Son can do nothing of his own accord, but only what he sees the Father doing. For **whatever things that One does, these things the Son does** likewise." (John 5:19) Jesus also said a few verses later, ""I can do nothing on my own. As I hear, I judge, and my judgment is just, because **I seek not my own will but the will of him who sent me**." (John 5:30) Imagine being a citizen of a kingdom, where the king of the most powerful country in the world allows his son, the prince, to voluntarily go off to fight in a war, sacrificing himself while willing doing the will of his father, living with the common troops, receiving no special favors, making the same sacrifices. How would you feel about your king and his son?—Philippians 2:5-8.

---

[2] Again, we are using the masculine father because it aligns with our analogy. Here again, we are very much appreciative to the mothers who made the sacrifice of letting their son defend our freedoms.

Appreciating the Ransom Sacrifice

This sacrifice requires much more than a mere thank you. We need to understand what the Father provided, and the Son volunteered for our salvation. (John 17:3) Then, we must play our implicit **trust in** that ransom. (Ac 3:19) Our love and appreciation must inspire us to dedicate our lives to the Father and the Son. (Matt. 7:21-23; 16:24) Jesus said, the only one who will receive eternal life, are those doing the will of the Father.

Matthew 7:21-23 Updated American Standard Version (UASV)

21 "Not everyone who says to me, 'Lord, Lord,' will enter the kingdom of heaven, but **the one who does the will of my Father** who is in heaven. 22 On that day many will say to me, 'Lord, Lord, did we not prophesy in your name, and cast out demons in your name, and do many mighty works in your name?' 23 And then I will declare to them, 'I never knew you; depart from me, you who practice lawlessness.'

The will of the Father and the Son is that all disciples proclaim the Word of God, teach, making more disciples. (Matt. 24:14; 28:19-20; Ac 1:8; Rom. 10:10-13) This is how we dedicate our lives, showing our love and our appreciation.

Our clause, "For God **so** loved the world," begins with οὕτως (*houtōs*), which is translated "so" may also be rendered "in this way" or "in this manner."[3] In other words,

---

[3] William Arndt, Frederick W. Danker, and Walter Bauer, *A Greek-English Lexicon of the New Testament and Other Early Christian Literature* (Chicago: University of Chicago Press, 2000), 741.

"in this way" refers to the *means* of Jesus offering himself as a ransom sacrifice. "In this way" God loved the world, God gave his only-begotten Son. The world here is not every human that has ever live or will ever live up unto the time of Jesus' return. The doctrine of universal salvation is not biblical. It refers to only those who are redeemable. "God loved the world **[of redeemable humankind]** so much that he gave his only-begotten Son, in order that everyone trusting in him will not be destroyed but have eternal life. Redeemable are those who are receptive to biblical truth. These ones have an open and receptive heart and accept the Gospel. Of course, with God's foreknowledge, he already knows everyone who will or will not be receptive to the Gospel. There is no conflict between God's foreknowledge and the free will of humankind. His seeing the future does not mean that he arranges or determines who will or will not accept the ransom sacrifice.

For God so loved the world (3:16). The Old Testament makes abundantly clear that God loves all that he has made, especially his people (e.g., Ex. 34:6–7; Deut. 7:7–8; Hos. 11:1–4, 8–11). In the Mishnah, R. Aqiba (c. A.D. 135) is quoted as saying, "Beloved is man for he was created in the image [of God].… Beloved are Israel for they were called children of God" (*m. 'Abot* 3:15). In these last days, God has demonstrated his love for the world through the gift of his one and only Son. Significantly, God's love extends not merely to Israel but to "the world," that is sinful humanity. Just as God's love encompasses the entire world, so Jesus made atonement for the sins of the whole world (1 John 2:2).[4]

---

4 Clinton E. Arnold, *Zondervan Illustrated Bible Backgrounds Commentary: John, Acts.*, vol. 2 (Grand Rapids, MI: Zondervan, 2002), 37.

CHAPTER 2 He Gave His Only-Begotten Son

John 3:16 Updated American Standard Version (UASV)

¹⁶ For God so loved the world that **he gave his only-begotten Son**, in order that everyone trusting in him will not be destroyed but have eternal life.

The Greatest Act of Love

At the death of Jesus Christ, a Roman centurion who was supervising the execution was astounded by the darkness that came before and the earthquake that followed, so much so, he uttered, "Truly this was the Son of God!" (Matt. 27:54) Clearly, Jesus was no normal man. This Roman centurion had just realized that he had helped to execute the only-begotten Son of God!

The Father had sent his Son to earth to be born as a human baby. Doing this meant that for over three decades, his Son was susceptible to the same pains and suffering as the rest of humankind, ending in the most gruesome torture and execution imaginable. The Father watched the divine human child Jesus grow into a perfect man. He watched as John the Baptist baptized the Son, where the Father said from heaven, "This is my Son, the beloved, in whom I am well pleased." (Matt. 3:17) The Father watched on as the Son faithfully carried out his will, fulfilling all of the prophecies, which certainly pleased the Father.–John 5:36; 17:4.

What, though, about Nisan 14, 33 A.D., did the Father feel, that night when Jesus was betrayed and arrested by a mob? How badly the Almighty God, who is love, felt as he watched his Son being deserted by his intimate friends, while illegally being placed on trial? How torn the Father's heart was, as he watched his Son being ridiculed, spat upon, and beat in the face with fists? What about when the Son was scourged, with his back being torn to ribbons? Then, in real time, watching from heaven the Father's Son was nailed hands and feet, to the cross, hanging there as the people reviled him. Then, the father watched on as his Son cried out the throes of agony. Finally, the Father watched on as his Son breathed his last breath.

Just as words fail us many times in life to convey our feelings, we must think of the feelings of the Father, the pain he suffered over the death of the Son, is likely beyond the words we humans can express. What we can convey is the motive behind the Father's allowing this ransom sacrifice to take place. Why did the Father feel it necessary to subject himself to going through such a painful sacrifice and have his Son suffer to such an extent? John 3:16 tells us, a verse so powerful that Martin Luther called it "the heart of the Bible, the Gospel in miniature." The motive behind such a sacrifice is love. The Father's gift to humanity, the sending of the Son to suffer a horrendous death for us, was the greatest act of love ever by the Father and the Son.

LOVE (Noun and Verb)

Old Testament

Verb: אָהַב (*'ahab*), GK 170 (S 157), 217x. *'ahab* is defined as "to love" or "to like." This verb is used to describe a variety of relationships in the OT.

(1) *'ahab* can be used to describe the marital relationship between a man and a woman. Moses writes of the love of Isaac and Rebekah: "Isaac brought her into the tent of his mother Sarah, and he married Rebekah. So she became his wife, and he loved her" (Gen 24:67). The culture of the OT was such that women were, at times, given to men in marriage. Love was not a prerequisite for such an event to take place (29:30). But true love could develop. The majority of uses of love in the Song of Songs have the female as subject, expressing love for a male.

Occasionally the word may be used to describe the act of making love, both within the law and outside of the law. The case of Isaac and Rebekah mentioned above probably involves intimate relations. The writer of 1 Kings, however, describes Solomon's love, many of whom were concubines: "But King Solomon loved many foreign women" (1 Ki. 11:1). These relationships were essentially political in nature, not emotional, and they certainly violated the spirit of Gen 2:24.

(2) *'ahab* can also describe the special love that exists between parents and their children. God recognizes the great love Abraham has for Isaac: "Take your son, your only son, Isaac, whom you love, and go to the region of Moriah" (Gen 22:2). In the context of parental love, however, love can also be divided. Isaac and Rebekah have sons, Esau and Jacob: "Isaac … loved Esau, but Rebekah loved Jacob" (25:28). Similarly, regarding Jacob, when his ten sons come to Egypt and unwittingly stand before Joseph, he questions them about their father and brother. They tell him of their aged father and describe their brother as "the only one of his mother's sons left, and his father loves him" (Gen 44:20). Note too that extended families can also experience such love, for in Ruth 4:15 we read about the love that a daughter-in-law expresses to her mother-in-law.

(3) *'ahab* likewise describes the deep love that friends can have for each other. This is not sexual in nature but attests to the deep abiding love that only God can provide. This is the love that Saul has for David (1 Sam. 16:21) and that David shares with Jonathan (18:1, 3). This can be called a familial or brotherly love.

(4) *'ahab* is also used with nonpersonal objects, such as love for: Jerusalem (Ps 122:6; Isa 66:10), special food items (Gen 27:4, 9, 14), discipline and knowledge (Prov 12:1), a long life (Ps 34:12), sleep (Prov 20:13), sin (17:19), pleasure (21:17), wine and oil (21:17), money (Eccl 5:10), and even (indirectly) death (Prov 8:36). Prominent in Proverbs is the love of wisdom, personified as a woman (Prov 4:6; 8:17, 21).

(5) The most important uses of *'ahab*, however, are in the religious sphere, being used 32x of God's love. Of these, two are of God's love for Jerusalem (Ps 78:68; 87:2). It is used 7x of God's loving righteousness, judgment, etc., and 23x of his loving Israel or particular individuals. On the other hand, *'ahab* is used 19x of human love for God, including loving his name, law, precepts, etc. Many of these occur in Deut. (e.g., 5:10; 6:5; 7:9; 10:12) or in contexts that appear to depend on this OT book (e.g., Jos 22:5; 23:11; 1 Ki. 3:3; Neh. 1:5).

Chief among these human uses is, of course, what is called the Shema (Deut 6:4–5), which is equivalent to Israel's confession of faith: "Hear, O Israel: The Lord our God, the Lord is one. Love the Lord your God with all your heart and with all your soul and with all your strength." Even today this is regularly cited in Jewish synagogues. Jesus picks up this text as "the first and greatest commandment" of the law of Moses, and he adds to it a second commandment like the first, which contains another use of *'ahab* (Lev 19:18), "Love your neighbor as yourself" (see Mt

22:37–40). These two commands summarize the entire law of God.

Why should Israel love the Lord their God? First and foremost is the fact that God is the only God there is, so any religious feelings must be directed to him alone. Moreover, this God has been active in the lives of his people, rescuing them from slavery in Egypt. Hence, love for God is a grateful response to his actions on their behalf (see especially Deut 11:1–12). Such love is expressed in obedience to his law (10:12–13; cf. Exod 20:6). Even that obedience requires the involvement of God in their lives (30:6); we cannot obey him in our own strength. It is for this reason that God's people actually love his law (e.g., Ps 119:113, 119, 127).

As far as God's own love itself is concerned, *'ahab* and the figure of marriage point behind the covenant to its motive and origin in the innermost personal being of God. His love for a special people is astounding—something unique in the ancient world, where the notion of God's love refers only to love of the gods for the king, not for the common people. In Hos 11:1 the OT comes close to saying that God is love. Note too that God's love for Israel is not based on any attractive feature of the nation, for they were often rebellious; rather, that love lies deep within his own being. Nevertheless, Israel can lay claim to that love because of God's faithfulness expressed by his oath (Deut 7:6–11).

In response to Israel's sin, God's love is expressed in judgment and forgiveness. Yet God's punishment of sin does not contradict his love; rather, it was because he loves so much that he takes Israel's sin seriously (cf., e.g., the "therefore" in Amos 3:2). As Prov 3:12 states, "the Lord disciplines those he loves, as a father the son he delights in," and note that God is Israel's Father (see Isa 63:16; Jer 31:9). But God's severe discipline is never separated from tenderness (cf. Hos 11:9). That God continues to love his stiff-necked people is almost beyond human comprehension. See *NIDNTT*, 1:277–99.

Noun: חֶסֶד (*ḥesed*) GK 2876 (S 2617), 249x. *ḥesed* is one of the richest, most theologically insightful terms in the OT. It denotes "kindness, love, loyalty, mercy," most poignantly employed in the context of the relationship between God and humans as well as between one human and another— the former relationship using the word three times as often as the latter.

ḥesed describes the special relationship God has with his covenantal people, and as such can be a difficult word to translate because it is so specific: "steadfast love" (ESV, RSV); "loyal love" or "covenant faithfulness" (NET); "unfailing love" (NLT); "loving-kindness" (KJV). In the context of human relationships, "kindness" characterizes familial relationships (Gen 20:13), friendships, and the relationship of a king to his subjects (1 Ki. 2:7). David and Jonathan's covenant binds them together with the expectation of showing mutual kindness to one another, even at the expense of other relationships (1 Sam. 20:8).

The Lord rebukes Israel because they have not shown faithfulness or "loyalty," and there is no knowledge of God in the land (Hos 4:1). Micah recounts the requirements of the Lord, "He has told you, O mortal, what is good; and what does the Lord require of you but to do justice, and to love *kindness*, and to walk humbly with your God?" (Mic 6:8). God requires such fidelity and kindness because he himself is kind and has shown kindness to his people.

Lot acknowledges the *ḥesed* shown to him by the two angelic beings who spared his life from the destruction of Sodom and Gomorrah (Gen 19:19). The Psalms effusively proclaim the steadfast love of God (e.g., Ps 31:7, 32:10; 57:3; 59:10; 94:18; 143:12). God's abiding love stabilizes (Ps

94:18, "When I thought, 'my foot is slipping,' your *steadfast love*, O Lord, held me up") and sustains life (119:88, "In your *steadfast love* spare my life, so that I may keep the decrees of your mouth").

God's great self-disclosure, when allowing his glory to pass before Moses, includes *ḥesed*. "The Lord, the Lord, a God merciful and gracious, slow to anger, and abounding in *steadfast love* and faithfulness, keeping *steadfast love* for the thousandth generation, forgiving iniquity and transgression and sin, yet by no means clearing the guilty" (Exod 34:6–8). The defining characteristic of God in covenantal relationship with his people is that he shows "kindness" to them. His wrath is short in contrast to his love: "For a brief moment I abandoned you, but with great compassion, I will gather you. In overflowing wrath, for a moment I hid my face from you, but with everlasting *love,* I will have compassion on you, says the Lord, your Redeemer" (Isa 54:7–8).

ḥesed defines God's rule: "Righteousness and justice are the foundation of your throne; *steadfast love* and faithfulness go before you" (Ps 89:14). In light of all that Micah prophesies in judgment of Israel's sin, he concludes in worshipful wonder, "Who is a God like you, pardoning iniquity and passing over the transgression of the remnant of your possession.... You will cast all our sins into the depths of the sea. You will show faithfulness to Jacob and unswerving *loyalty* to Abraham, as you have sworn to our ancestors from the days of old" (Mic 7:19–20). See *NIDOTTE*, 2:211–18.

New Testament

Verb: ἀγαπάω (*agapaō*), GK *26* (*S 25*), 143x. *agapaō* is one of four Gk. verbs meaning "to love." In secular Greek especially before the time of Christ, it was a colorless word without any great depth of meaning, used frequently as a synonym of *erōs* (sexual love) and *phileō* (the general term for love). If it had any nuance, it was the idea of love for the sake of its object. Perhaps because of its neutrality of meaning and perhaps because of this slight nuance of meaning, the biblical writers picked *agapaō* to describe many forms of human love (e.g., husband and wife, Eph 5:25, 28, 33) and, most importantly, God's undeserved love for the unlovely. In other words, its meaning comes not from the Greek but from the biblical understanding of God's love.

A biblical definition of love starts with God, never with us (1 Jn. 4:9–10). God is love itself; it is his character that defines love. Because he is love (4:8, using the related noun *agapē*), he acts with love toward an undeserving world (Jn 3:16; 1 Jn. 3:1, 16), to save them from their sins and reconcile them to himself (Rom 5:8). The pure and perfect love of God is typified in the love relationship between God the Father and God the Son, which Jesus shows to his disciples (Jn 17:26).

In response, people are to love God. "Dear friends, let us love one another, for love comes from God. Everyone who loves has been born of God and knows God. Whoever does not love does not know God, because God is love" (1 Jn. 4:7–8). They are in fact to love God above everything else, which is the greatest commandment (Mk 12:30, 33), and then to love one another (Mt 19:19; 22:39; Mk 12:31; Rom 13:8; 1 Jn. 3:11, 23), especially their spiritual family (Gal 6:10; 1 Jn. 2:10).

If a person loves God, he or she will also love other people (Gal 5:6; 1 Thess. 3:6; 1 Jn. 4:20). Loving the other person is an outflow of God's love for you ("A new command I give you: Love one another. As I have loved you, so you must love one another," Jn 13:34; cf. 15:12; 1

Jn. 4:11) and sums up the entire law (Rom 13:7; Gal 5:14) and is the "royal law" (Jas 2:8). "Anyone who does not do what is right is not a child of God; nor is anyone who does not love his brother" (1 Jn. 3:10). Our love toward Christ is demonstrated by our obedience to his teachings (Jn 14:21, 15, 21, 23; 15:10; 1 Jn. 2:5; 5:3; 2 Jn. 6). In return, this obedience invokes the blessing, of God's love for us (Jn 14:21). No wonder that love stands at the head of the list of the fruits of the Spirit (Gal 5:22) and is the greatest of all that will last for eternity (1 Cor. 13:13, both using the noun *agapê*).

But disciples are not only to love God and fellow believers; they are to love all people (1 Cor. 16:14; 1 Thess. 3:12; 2 Pet. 1:7) as especially their enemies. "But I tell you: Love your enemies and pray for those who persecute you" (Mt 5:44; cf. Lk 6:35).

The very foundation of salvation is grounded in the realization that God's unmerited love toward us is greater than any other power—including death (Rom 8:37–39; 1 Cor. 15:55–57). See *NIDNTT-A*, 5–7.

Verb: φιλέω (*phileō*), GK *5797* (*S 5368*), 25x. *phileō* is the common word in classical Gk. for showing love, affection, hospitality, etc. It comes into English in many words such as "*Phil*adelphia" (the "city of brotherly love"). To make firm distinctions between *phileō* love and *agapaō* love is incorrect, for the meanings of the two words overlap. The word can also mean "kiss."

phileō is used in the Bible to describe the tender affection that God the Father has toward his Son, Jesus Christ: "For the Father *loves* the Son and shows him all he does" (Jn 5:20). But it is also used for our love for God. Jesus uses *phileō* to warn those who have more affection for family than for him: "Anyone who *loves* his father or mother more than me is not worthy of me; anyone who *loves* his son or daughter more than me is not worthy of me" (Mt 10:37). Paul warns the Corinthians, "If anyone does not *love* the Lord—a curse be on him" (1 Cor. 6:22).

phileō can also be used for relationships among human beings, whether in a positive or negative framework. Of Lazarus, Jesus was told, "Lord, the one *you love* is sick" (Jn 11:3; cf. v 36). Judas "kisses" as the sign of betrayal (Mt 26:48; Mk 14:44; Lk 22:47). Paul uses *phileō* to speak of the love that God's people have toward one another: "Greet those who *love* us in the faith" (Tit 3:15). John uses the word to describe the framework in which God chastens his children: "Those whom I *love* I rebuke and discipline" (Rev 3:19).

phileō can even be used of love for nonhuman things. John uses *phileō* to describe ungodly people who "*love* and practice falsehood" (Rev 22:15) Hypocrites "*love* to pray standing in the synagogues and on the street corners to be seen by men" (Mt 6:5).

Love is one of the characteristics that separate disciples from the world. If a disciple loves his life in the sense of desperately hanging on to it, he will ironically lose that which he loves; but if a disciple hates his life (i.e., gives it up for Christ), then he will keep his life for all eternity (Jn 12:25). If disciples were still of this world, the world "would love" them; but because Jesus chose them out of the world, they are hated (15:19). But the wonderful news is that God the Father himself loves those who love Jesus and believe that he came from God (16:27).

In Jn 21:15–27, some people make a distinction between the two words for love, *agapaō* and *phileō*. But these words do not have distinctly separate meanings, and John is famous for using virtual synonyms without any difference in meaning; he often switches between words merely for the sake of variety. Also, it makes no sense for Jesus to switch meanings from *agapaō* to *phileō* in the third question since Peter has been answering with *phileō*. Jesus' threefold question is meant to balance Peter's threefold denial at the time of Jesus' trial. The fluctuation of synonyms is also seen in the words for "feed"/"tend" and "lambs"/"sheep." See *NIDNTT-A*, 590–91.

Noun: ἀγάπη (*agapē*), GK *27* (*S 26*), 116x. *agapē* signifies the true and pure love of God to his dear Son (Jn 17:26), to his people (Gal 6:10), and to a depraved humanity that is in rebellion against him (Jn 3:16; Rom 5:8). In fact, the Bible declares that the very nature of God can be defined as love (1 Jn. 4:8, 16). We can see that God is love, regardless of our situation in life; Heb 12:6 explains that even though we may be under the correction of God, the correction is always guided by love. It is the love of God that prompts our obedience to him. Jesus told his disciples, "Whoever has my commandments and obeys them, he is the one who loves me. He who loves me will be loved by my Father, and I too will love him and show myself to him" (Jn 14:21, using the related verb *agapaô*).

agapē encompasses the mind, emotions, and will of the individual because it comes from God. As such, we are to live the life of love as demonstrated by the Lord Jesus Christ himself (Eph 5:2). Paul tells us, "The fruit of the Spirit is love" (Gal 5:22); it is only by the indwelling of the Holy Spirit of God that we can internalize and realize the love that God has for us. This type of godly love compels us to look for unmet needs among our fellow human beings. It is godly compulsion (2 Cor. 5:14), which brings us to a point where the world no longer sees us, but rather Christ in us. This idea prompted the translators of the KJV to translate *agapē* as "charity" (see, e.g., 1 Cor. 13). Derived from the

Latin word *caritas*, charity is characterized in the KJV as an out-showing of God's love and benevolence toward humanity. Further examination of 1 Cor. 13 reveals an inseparable relationship between faith, hope, and love (1 Cor. 13:13), yet the apostle affirms the supremacy of love. John explains that as the love of the church increases, God will strengthen the hearts of those in the church so that they "will be blameless and holy in the presence of our God and Father when our Lord Jesus comes with all his holy ones" (1 Thess. 3:13).

God's people are exhorted to be cautious where they place their love. "Do not love the world or anything in the world. If anyone loves the world, the love of the Father is not in him. For everything in the world—the cravings of sinful man, the lust of his eyes and the boasting of what he has and does—comes not from the Father but from the world" (1 Jn. 2:15). Paul warns young Timothy that "the love of money is a root of all kinds of evils," and as a result "some have wandered away from the faith and pierced themselves with many pangs" (1 Tim. 6:10).

agapē is also used to describe an early Christian "love feast" or fellowship meal. Paul links this meal with the Lord's Supper (1 Cor. 11), but eventually it become a celebration all its own (Jude 12; 2 Pet. 2:13). The meal was significant to the life of the church insofar as it typified what the church represented. It was the church's direct response to the command of the Lord Jesus Christ to love one another. This *agapē* served to undergird the *koinōnia* (see fellowship) that the church experienced.

Lastly, *agapē* is a beautiful word picture of sacrificial love. It is expressed in the fact that "while we were still sinners, Christ died for us" (Rom 5:8). As such, *agapē* can be defined as unmerited and unwavering love. God is the originator of this love, and it can only be experienced by one who truly knows God and has received his Son as Lord and Savior. The ultimate expression of God's unmitigated love is the Lord Jesus Christ on Calvary's cross.[5]

---

[5] William D. Mounce, *Mounce's Complete Expository Dictionary of Old & New Testament Words* (Grand Rapids, MI: Zondervan, 2006), 424–429.

CHAPTER 3 In Order That Everyone Trusting In Him

John 3:16 Updated American Standard Version (UASV)

¹⁶ For God so loved the world that he gave his only-begotten Son, **in order that everyone trusting in him** will not be destroyed but have eternal life.

Trusting In Jesus Christ

If we are to please the Father and the Son, we must evidence trust in the promises found in God's Word. Such trust should move us to become exemplary Christians. The apostle Peter wrote, "Now for this very reason also, applying all diligence, **in your faith supply virtue**, and in your virtue, knowledge, and in your knowledge, self-control, and in your self-control, perseverance, and in your perseverance, godliness, and in your godliness, brotherly kindness, and in your brotherly kindness, love." (2 Peter 1:5-7) Here Peter has given us a list of Christian personality traits that we do well to apply in our lives. It is unrealistic to try to make changes on each trait in the list at one time. What we could do is look at one trait at a time. Look it up in a Bible dictionary or a word study dictionary, to see what all is involved in that trait. If we are falling short in some way, we need to make needed changes to align ourselves. After we have that trait incorporated in our personality, we move onto the next, and so on. Remember, though, we are imperfect, and we will never live up to any Christian trait perfectly.

Peter said that virtue, knowledge, self-control, perseverance, godliness, brotherly kindness, and love are to be supplied to one another and our faith. These qualities must be a foundational part of our faith. For example, virtue is not a Christian quality that exists outside of our faith. *Vine's Complete Expository Dictionary* says, "Virtue is enjoined as an essential quality in the exercise of faith."[6] Being virtuous means that we are walking with God, i.e., follow a life-course based on the Word of God.

Why must **knowledge** be added to our faith? We are mentally bent toward evil (Gen. 6:8; 8:21), our inner person is treacherous (Jer. 17:9), and we have a sinful nature, as we walk through Satan's wicked world. As we face these challenges to our faith, we need to continually keep adding knowledge and refining the knowledge that we have so that we can distinguish right from wrong. (Heb. 5:14) As we continuously, regularly study God's Word over the years, we apply the Bible in our daily lives, which gives us a biblical worldview, and life experience, so we enlarge our knowledge. This will maintain our faith, enabling us to remain virtuous.—Proverbs 2:6-8; James 1:5-8.

If we are to face the trials of Satan's world boldly, we need to add self-control to or knowledge. The Greek (*egkrateia*) denotes "to exercise complete control over one's desires and actions, 'to control oneself, to exercise self-

---

[6] W. E. Vine, Merrill F. Unger, and William White Jr., *Vine's Complete Expository Dictionary of Old and New Testament Words* (Nashville, TN: T. Nelson, 1996), 661.

control, self-control.'"[7] We need to show restraint in thought, word, and conduct. If we are determined in applying our self-control, we will add perseverance. This perseverance (*hypomonē*) is the "capacity to continue to bear up under difficult circumstances, 'endurance, being able to endure.'[8]

In our perseverance, we need to add godliness (*eusebeia*), which is devotion, a reverence, worship, and service we give to God. This "denotes that piety which, characterized by a Godward attitude, does that which is well-pleasing to Him."[9] In your godliness, we need to add brotherly kindness, which is "affection for one's fellow believer in Christ.[10] Finally, in our brotherly kindness, we must add love, which is having "love for someone or something, based on sincere appreciation and high regard"[11] One of the ways we express this love is our proclaiming God's Word, teaching, and making disciples.–Matthew 24:14; 28:19-20; Acts 1:8.

---

[7] Johannes P. Louw and Eugene Albert Nida, *Greek-English Lexicon of the New Testament: Based on Semantic Domains* (New York: United Bible Societies, 1996), 750.

[8] Johannes P. Louw and Eugene Albert Nida, *Greek-English Lexicon of the New Testament: Based on Semantic Domains* (New York: United Bible Societies, 1996), 307.

[9] W. E. Vine, Merrill F. Unger, and William White Jr., *Vine's Complete Expository Dictionary of Old and New Testament Words* (Nashville, TN: T. Nelson, 1996), 272.

[10] Johannes P. Louw and Eugene Albert Nida, *Greek-English Lexicon of the New Testament: Based on Semantic Domains* (New York: United Bible Societies, 1996), 292.

[11] Johannes P. Louw and Eugene Albert Nida, *Greek-English Lexicon of the New Testament: Based on Semantic Domains* (New York: United Bible Societies, 1996), 292.

Exegetical Commentary on 2 Peter 1:5-7

Contextual Background

Before we delve into the individual verses, it's crucial to establish the context in which these verses appear. The Apostle Peter, in his second letter, addresses a beleaguered Christian audience facing false teachings and moral decline. The overarching theme of this epistle is the acquisition and application of divine knowledge as a safeguard against apostasy.

2 Peter 1:5

"Now for this very reason also, applying all diligence, in your faith supply virtue..."

Peter begins by highlighting the urgency ("for this very reason") of applying "all diligence" in the Christian walk. The Greek word "spoudē," often translated as diligence, connotes earnestness and a form of zealous effort. The imperative here is unmistakable: Christian living requires serious, committed effort.

Peter advises the addition of "virtue" (Greek: "aretē") to faith. Virtue here is understood as moral excellence or uprightness and is the natural outgrowth of a faith that is alive and active.

2 Peter 1:6

"...and in your virtue, knowledge, and in your knowledge, self-control, and in your self-control, perseverance..."

Peter lists additional virtues that should be sequentially added to one's life. First, he mentions "knowledge" (Greek:

"gnōsis"). This is not merely factual knowledge but experiential knowledge of God that informs the moral life.

Next comes "self-control" (Greek: "enkrateia"). This virtue is vital for moral and ethical living, as it implies mastery over sinful desires and impulses. The presence of self-control is a hallmark of mature Christian character.

The sequence continues with "perseverance" (Greek: "hypomonē"). This signifies patient endurance, particularly during trials and sufferings. Peter, who himself faced immense persecution, underscores the importance of enduring hardships in the Christian walk.

2 Peter 1:7

"...and in your perseverance, godliness, and in your godliness, brotherly kindness, and in your brotherly kindness, love."

Godliness (Greek: "eusebeia") is next in this sequence of virtues. This entails a piety or reverence towards God, reflecting a life in harmony with God's will.

Following godliness is "brotherly kindness" (Greek: "philadelphia"). This virtue extends the Christian's piety towards fellow believers, indicating a community-centric aspect of Christian living.

Finally, Peter culminates this list with "love" (Greek: "agapē"). This is the highest form of Christian virtue, an unconditional, sacrificial love that reflects the love of God Himself. It's the cornerstone of Christian ethics and is inclusive not just of believers but of all humanity.

Summary and Theological Implications

The virtues Peter lists aren't meant to be standalone qualities but are interconnected, each building on the previous. This is not a call to legalistic piety but a guideline for spiritual maturation, supported by the preceding context of divine empowerment (2 Peter 1:3-4).

Peter's model also reflects a balanced Christian life that requires both divine enablement and human effort ("applying all diligence"). It presents a comprehensive path to Christian maturity, starting from the foundation of faith and culminating in the pinnacle of Christian virtue—agape love. This trajectory outlines the transformative power of true, experiential knowledge of God, safeguarding the believer from both moral decline and false teachings.

In essence, Peter offers a robust, sequenced guide for Christian development, echoing Paul's theological emphasis on the sanctification process, which is both immediate and ongoing. This guide is not only theological but also immensely practical, offering concrete steps for ethical and spiritual maturity.

As loyal servants of the Father and disciples of the Son, we have faith that God's Word is true, and if we accurately understand it, we will possess that absolute truth, knowing that all promises will be fulfilled. If we are to walk with our God faithfully trusting in his Son, we must add to our faith virtue, knowledge, self-control, perseverance, godliness, brotherly kindness, and love.

CHAPTER 4 Will Not Be Destroyed

John 3:16 Updated American Standard Version (UASV)

¹⁶ For God so loved the world that he gave his only-begotten Son, in order that everyone trusting in him **will not be destroyed** but have eternal life.

The Greek (*apollymai*) has the primary meaning destroy, ruin, or cause destruction. It has the sense of being without life because God condemns us. The *Complete Expository Dictionary* says, "to experience destruction, "to perish." Objects can perish (Mt 9:17; Mk 2:22; Lk 5:37), as well as people. The Greek middle voice sometimes indicates physical death. The disciples used this word when they thought they would drown, "Lord, save us, we are *perishing!*" (Mt 8:25; cf. Mk 4:38; Lk 8:24). Jesus warns, "All who draw the sword will *die* by the sword" (Mt 26:52). It can also signify the destruction meted out in divine judgment: "None of them has *perished* except the son of destruction" (Jn 17:12; cf. 10:28). The "perishing" destiny is set in contrast to eternal life: "For God so loved the world that he gave his one and only Son, that whoever believes in him shall not *perish* but have eternal life" (Jn 3:16)."¹²

On this clause, Andreas J. Köstenberger writes, "In John, likewise, there is no middle ground: believing in the Son (resulting in eternal life) or refusing to believe (resulting

---

¹² William D. Mounce, *Mounce's Complete Expository Dictionary of Old & New Testament Words* (Grand Rapids, MI: Zondervan, 2006), 423.

in destruction) are the only options. Since "perish" is contrasted with "*eternal* life," it stands to reason that perishing is eternal as well."[13] Whether we receive eternal life, therefore, depends on how you respond to God's love.

Elmer Town writes, "Every Christian has eternal life, this is why Jesus came (John 3:16). The basis for eternal life is the resurrection. "Jesus said ... I am the resurrection and the life; he that believeth in me, though he were dead, yet shall he live" (John 11:25). Again Paul stated, "The gift of God is eternal life through Jesus Christ our Lord" (Rom. 6:23). Jesus said, 'He that heareth my word, and believeth on him that sent me, hath everlasting life, and shall not come into condemnation, but is passed from death unto life' (John 5:24)."[14]

Passing Over from Death to Life

John 5:24 Updated American Standard Version (UASV)

[24] Truly, truly, I say to you, whoever hears my word and believes him who sent me has eternal life. He does not come into judgment, but has passed from death to life.

Regeneration is God restoring and renewing somebody morally or spiritually, where the Christian receives a new quality of life. This one goes from the road to death over to the path of life. (John 5:24) Here he becomes a new person, with a new personality, having

---

[13] Andreas J. Köstenberger, *John*, Baker Exegetical Commentary on the New Testament (Grand Rapids, MI: Baker Academic, 2004), 129–130.

[14] Towns, Elmer. AMG Concise Bible Doctrines (AMG Concise Series) (Kindle Locations 2968-2971). AMG Publishers. Kindle Edition.

removed the old person. (Eph. 4:20-24) **This does not mean** that the imperfection is gone, and the sinful desires are removed, but that he now has the mind of Christ, the Spirit and the Word of God to gain control over his thinking and his fleshly desires. Therefore, if one has truly experienced a conversion, it will be evident by the changes in one's new personality from the old personality, his life, and his actions. If this is the case, he will be fulfilling the words of Jesus, "let your light shine before others, so that they may see your good works and give glory to your Father who is in heaven." (Matt. 5:16)

Can we see one as truly a man of faith, a committed Christian, who attends the meetings, but never carries out any personal study, never shares the gospel with another, never helps his spiritual brothers or sisters (physically, materially, mentally, or spiritually), nor helps his neighbor, or any of the other things one would find within a man of faith? James had something to say about this back in chapter 1:26-27, "If anyone thinks he is religious and does not bridle his tongue but deceives his heart, this person's religion is worthless. Religion that is pure and undefiled before God, the Father, is this: to visit orphans and widows in their affliction, and to keep oneself unstained from the world." One who does not possess real faith, will not help the poor, he will not separate himself from worldly pursuits, he will favor those that he can benefit from (the powerful and wealthy), and ignore those that he cannot make gains from (orphans and widows), he will not know the love of God, nor his mercy.—James. 2:8-9, 13.

Titus 3:5 Updated American Standard Version (UASV)

⁵ he saved us, not by deeds of righteousness that we have done, but because of his mercy, through the washing of regeneration and renewal by the Holy Spirit,

The Greek word (*palingenesia*) means to a renewal or rebirth of a new life in Christ, by the Holy Spirit. Jesus told Nicodemus, "Unless someone is born of ... Spirit, he is not able to enter into the kingdom of God." (John 3:5). At the moment a person is converted, he is regenerated or renewed, passing over from death to life eternal. Jesus explains this at John 5:24, "the one who hears my word and who believes the one who sent me has eternal life, and does not come into judgment, but has passed from death into life." The principal feature of the rebirth of a new life in Christ, by the Holy Spirit, regeneration, is the passing over from death to life eternal.

At that point, the Spirit dwells within this newly regenerated one. From the time of Adam and Eve, God has desired to dwell with man. God fellowshipped with Adam in the Garden of Eden. After Adam's rebellion, he chose faithful men, to walk with him in their life course, to communicate with them. Enoch, Noah, and Abraham walked with God. In the Hebrew language, the tabernacle is called *mishkan* meaning "dwelling place." In both the tabernacle and the temple, God was represented as dwelling with the people in the Most Holy. He also dwelt with the people through the Son, "And the Word became flesh and dwelt among us, and we have seen his glory, glory as of the only Son from the Father, full of grace and truth." (John 1:14) After Jesus' ascension, God dwelt among the Christians, by way of the Holy Spirit, in the body of each individual Christian, which begins at conversion.

On John 3:16, Gregory A. Boyd and Paul R. Eddy write, "Because he loves all, he wants everyone to be saved.

God takes no delight in the destruction of any wicked person but rather desires all to repent (Ezek. 18: 23, 32; 33: 11). In the words of the apostle Peter, God is "not wanting any to perish, but all to come to repentance" (2 Pet. 3: 9, emphasis added). He "desires everyone to be saved and to come to the knowledge of the truth" (1 Tim. 2: 4, emphasis added). Indeed, in explicit contradiction to the notion that Jesus died only for select individuals, Scripture tells us that God desires to be "the Savior of all people" (1 Tim. 4: 10) and thus that Jesus died as "the atoning sacrifice . . . for the sins of the whole world" (1 John 2: 2; cf. Heb. 2: 9). Second, God loves everyone, but love is a two-way street. While love is who God is, humans are contingent beings who thus must choose it. This is why throughout Scripture God calls people to make decisions. Beginning in the Garden of Eden and extending through the book of Revelation, God sets before us "life and death," all the while pleading with us to "choose life that you . . . may live" (Deut. 30: 19; cf. Josh. 24: 15; Acts 17: 30– 31). In the New Testament, this choice is the choice to place one's trust in Jesus Christ or to reject him. Over and over we read the call to "believe in the Lord Jesus Christ" with the promise that if you do so "you will be saved" (Acts 16: 31; cf. John 3: 16; Acts 2: 21; Rom. 10: 13). The invitation is offered to everyone with the hope that all will choose to accept it."[15]

---

[15] Gregory A. Boyd; Paul R. Eddy. Across the Spectrum: Understanding Issues in Evangelical Theology (pp. 154-155). Baker Publishing Group. Kindle Edition.

CHAPTER 5 But Have Eternal Life

John 3:16 Updated American Standard Version (UASV)

16 For God so loved the world that he gave his only-begotten Son, in order that everyone trusting in him will not be destroyed but **have eternal life**.

The Greek phrase (*zōē aiōnios*) "life eternal" or "eternal life" means an eternal life of an unlimited duration. It has the sense of continuing forever or indefinitely. Let us look at a couple of other terms that will add to our understanding.

The Greek word *athanasia* is formed by the negative prefix "a" followed by a form of the word for "death" (*thanatos*). Thus, the basic meaning is "deathlessness," and refers to the quality of life that is enjoyed, its endlessness and indestructibility. This is the quality or state of never dying. The *Dictionary of Biblical Languages with Semantic Domains* supports this when it says it is "a state of not being able to die or degenerate."[16] (1 Cor. 15:53-54, 1 Tim. 6:16) The Greek word *aphtharsia*, meaning "incorruption," refers to that which cannot break down or decay, that which is imperishable.–Rom. 2:7; 1 Cor. 15:42, 50, 53; Eph. 6:24; 2 Tim. 1:10.

---

[16] James Swanson, *Dictionary of Biblical Languages with Semantic Domains: Greek (New Testament)* (Oak Harbor: Logos Research Systems, Inc., 1997).

Immortality (Gr, *athanasia*; deathlessness) means indestructible, "the state of not being subject to death (that which will never die)."[17] This means that Adam was not created inherently immortal, possessing deathlessness, but rather the opportunity at endless life. This is quite amazing, considering the fact that even God's angels do not possess immortality, even though they possess spirit bodies, not carnal ones. (1 Cor. 15:53; 1 Tim. 6:16) Kenneth O. Gangel writes, "The verb **perish** speaks of eternal death in contrast to eternal life. It represents the opposite of preservation since death is the opposite of life. Those who refuse God's gift are alienated from Him without hope for both the present and the future. A person need not sin blatantly to perish. One may simply fail to act positively in receiving God's gift."[18]

New Heavens and New Earth?

The Bible teaches that the universe, created by God, will eventually be redeemed from the influence of sin. This renewed universe is referred to as "the new heavens and the new earth." In the Old Testament, particularly in Isaiah, the kingdom of God is often described as a renewed earth (Isaiah 65:17; 66:22). The authors of the Old Testament had only a vague understanding of what this renewal would involve, but they did express that human destiny is fundamentally earthly.

---

[17] Johannes P. Louw and Eugene Albert Nida, *Greek-English Lexicon of the New Testament: Based on Semantic Domains* (New York: United Bible Societies, 1996), 267.

[18] Kenneth O. Gangel, *John*, vol. 4, Holman New Testament Commentary (Nashville, TN: Broadman & Holman Publishers, 2000), 55.

The New Testament clarifies this view. Jesus talks about the "renewal" of the world in Matthew 19:28. Peter refers to a "restoration of all things" in Acts 3:21. Paul writes in Romans 8:18-21 that the universe will be liberated from its current fallen state. Peter also confirms this by describing the new heavens and new earth as places characterized by righteousness (2 Peter 3:13). Finally, the Book of Revelation provides a vivid depiction of this new universe, reaffirming God's promise to make everything new (Revelation 21:1-8).

The new heavens and the new earth will serve as the culmination of God's original intent for creation. This renewed universe will be completely under God's rule and will be the ultimate realization of His redemptive plan, where God will dwell among humans (Revelation 21:3).

It's important to note that the Bible's view of our future is not some ghostly, immaterial existence but a physical life on a renewed earth. In other words, spiritual fulfillment does not exclude physical creation; rather, it will be fully realized in a renewed and perfected world.

Scholars have debated whether this future state involves a renewal of the existing universe or a complete destruction and re-creation from scratch. Both perspectives have their supporters and can be backed by various scriptural passages. For example, Matthew 19:28, Acts 3:21, and Romans 8:18-21 suggest a renewal, while 2 Peter 3:7-13 leans more toward a complete re-creation. The most balanced view seems to be that the future state will involve both continuity and discontinuity: the universe will be renewed, but this transformation will be so thorough that it will essentially usher in a radically new state of existence.

Heavenly Hope

Revelation 14:1-4 Updated American Standard Version (UASV)

14 Then I looked, and behold, the Lamb was standing on Mount Zion, and with him **one hundred and forty-four thousand**, having his name and the name of his Father written on their foreheads. ²And I heard a voice from heaven, like the sound of many waters and like the sound of loud thunder, and the voice which I heard was like the sound of harpists playing on their harps. ³And t**hey sang a new song**[19] before the throne and before the four living creatures and the elders; and **no one could learn the song except the one hundred and forty-four thousand who had been purchased from the earth**. ⁴These are the ones who have not been defiled with women, for they are virgins. These are the ones who follow the Lamb wherever He goes. These have been purchased from among men as first fruits to God and to the Lamb.

> The whole of chapter 14 is proleptic. As a summary of the Millennium (20:4–6), the first five verses feature the Lamb in place of the beast, the Lamb's followers with His and the Father's seal in place of the beast's followers with the mark of the beast, and the divinely controlled Mount Zion

---

[19] TR WH NU have ἄδουσιν [ὡς] ᾠδὴν καινήν

("they sing, as it were, a new song"), which is supported by A C 051 Majᵃ. However, all modern-day English versions have the variant reading αδουσιν ωδην καινην ("they sing a new song"), which is supported by P⁴⁷ P¹¹⁵ᵛⁱᵈ ℵ P 046 2053 2344.

in place of the pagan-controlled earth (Alford, Moffatt, Kiddle).[20]

Revelation 7:4 Updated American Standard Version (UASV)

[4] And I heard the number of the ones who were sealed, one hundred forty-four thousand sealed from every tribe of the sons of Israel:

> Various efforts have sought to determine the significance of the number 144,000. An understanding of the number as symbolical divides it into three of its multiplicands, 12 × 12 × 1000. From the symbolism of the three it is concluded that the number indicates fixedness and fullest completeness.[21] Twelve, a number of the tribes, is both squared and multiplied by a thousand. This is a twofold way of emphasizing completeness (Mounce). It thus affirms the full number of God's people to be brought through tribulation (Ladd). The symbolic approach points out the impossibility of taking the number literally. It is simply a vast number, less than a number indefinitely great (cf. 7:9), but greater than a large number designedly finite (e.g., 1,000, Rev. 20:2) (Lee). Other occurrences of the numerical components that are supposedly symbolic are also pointed out, 12 thousand in Rev. 21:16, 12 in Rev. 22:2, and 24, a multiple of 12, in Rev. 4:4. This is done to enhance the case for symbolism (Johnson). Though

---

[20] Robert L. Thomas, Revelation 8-22: An Exegetical Commentary (Chicago: Moody Publishers, 1995), 189.

[21] Alford, Greek Testament, 4:624; Charles, Revelation, 1:206; Lenski, Revelation, p. 154.

admittedly ingenious, the case for symbolism is exegetically weak. The principal reason for the view is a predisposition to make the 144,000 into a group representative of the church with which no possible numerical connection exists. No justification can be found for understanding the simple statement of fact in v. 4 as a figure of speech. It is a definite number in contrast with the indefinite number of 7:9. If it is taken symbolically, no number in the book can be taken literally. As God reserved 7,000 in the days of Ahab (1 Kings 19:18; Rom. 11:4), He will reserve 144,000 for Himself during the future Great Tribulation.[22] (Thomas, Revelation 1-7: An Exegetical Commentary 1992, 473-74)

These ones are made up of those under the new covenant, the Law of Christ, those **called out of natural Israel**, and the new Israelites, also known as the Israel of God. They are a chosen number that is to reign with Jesus as kings, priests, and judges. Therefore, we ask, what is the other hope?

---

[22] Bullinger, Apocalypse, p. 282. Geyser is correct in observing that the predominant concern of the Apocalypse is "the restoration [on earth] of the twelve tribes of Israel, their restoration as a twelve-tribe kingdom, in a renewed and purified city of David, under the rule of the victorious 'Lion of the Tribe of Judah, the Root of David' (5:5; 22:16)" (Albert Geyser, "The Twelve Tribes in Revelation: Judean and Judeo Christian Apocalypticism," NTS 23, no. 3 [July 1982]: 389). He is wrong, however, in his theory that this belief characterized the Judean church only and was not shared by Gentile Christianity spearheaded by Paul (ibid., p. 390).

The New Earth: The Earthly Hope

In the O[ld] T[estament] the kingdom of God is usually described in terms of a redeemed earth; this is especially clear in the book of Isaiah, where the final state of the universe is already called new heavens and a new earth (65:17; 66:22) The nature of this renewal was perceived only very dimly by OT authors, but they did express the belief that a humans ultimate destiny is an earthly one.[23] This vision is clarified in the N[ew] T[estament]. Jesus speaks of the "renewal" of the world (Matt 19:28), Peter of the restoration of all things (Acts 3:21). Paul writes that the universe will be redeemed by God from its current state of bondage (Rom. 8:18-21). This is confirmed by Peter, who describes the new heavens and the new earth as the Christian's hope (2 Pet. 3:13). Finally, the book of Revelation includes a glorious vision of the end of the present universe and the creation of a new universe, full of righteousness and the presence of God. The vision is confirmed by God in the awesome declaration: "I am making everything new!" (Rev. 21:1-8)

The new heavens and the new earth will be the renewed creation that will fulfill the purpose for which God created the universe. It will be characterized by the complete rule of God and by

---

[23] It is unwise to speak of the written Word of God as if it were of human origin, saying, 'OT authors express the belief,' when what was written is the meaning and message of what God wanted to convey by means of the human author.

the full realization of the final goal of redemption: "Now the dwelling of God is with men" (Rev. 21:3).

The fact that the universe will be created anew[24] shows that God's goals for humans is not an ethereal and disembodied existence, but a bodily existence on a perfected earth. The scene of the beatific vision is the new earth. The spiritual does not exclude the created order and will be fully realized only within a perfected creation. (Elwell 2001, 828-29)

What have we learned so far in this article? God created the earth to be inhabited, to be filled with perfect humans, who are over the animals, and under the sovereignty of God. (Gen 1:28; 2:8, 15; Ps 104:5; 115:16; Eccl 1:4) Sin did not dissuade God from his plans (Isa. 45:18); hence, he has saved redeemable humankind by Jesus' ransom sacrifice. It seems that the Bible offers two hopes to redeemed humans, (1) a heavenly hope, or (2) an earthly hope. It also seems that those with heavenly hope are limited in number and are going to heaven to rule with Christ as kings, priests, and judges either on the earth or over the earth from heaven. It seems that those with earthly hope will receive eternal life here on a paradise earth as originally intended.

---

[24] Creating anew does not mean complete destruction followed by a re-creation but rather a renewal of the present universe.

Edward D. Andrews

CHAPTER 6
Everlasting Happiness
Awaits the Godly Ones

John 3:16 Updated American Standard Version (UASV)

16 For God so loved the world that he gave his only-begotten Son, in order that everyone trusting in him will not be destroyed but have eternal life.

The Creator of the heavens and the earth has bestowed on his people a wonderful give, the hope of everlasting happiness. All **godly ones** have the resurrection hope. (John 5:28-29, see next chapter)

He has also given us the work of sharing this good news of the kingdom with the entire inhabited earth. (Matt 24:14; Mark 13:10) We have the privilege of teaching and making disciples of all, who are receptive to accepting the Son as their personal savior. (Matt. 28:19-20, Ac 1:8) Being one of Jesus' witnesses is a privilege and honor.

Evangelism is the work of a Christian evangelist, of which all true Christians are obligated to partake to some extent, which seeks to persuade other people to become Christian, especially by sharing the basics of the Gospel, but also the deeper message of biblical truths. Today the Gospel is almost an unknown, so what does the Christian evangelist do? **Preevangelism** is laying a foundation for those who have no knowledge of the Gospel, giving them background information, so that they are able to grasp what they are hearing. The Christian evangelist is preparing their mind and heart so that they will be receptive to the biblical truths. In many ways, this is known as apologetics.

Christian Apologetics [Greek: *apologia*, "verbal defense, speech in defense"] is a field of **Christian theology** which endeavors to offer a reasonable and sensible basis for the **Christian faith**, defending the faith against objections. It is reasoning from the Scriptures, explaining and proving, as one instructs in sound doctrine, many times having to overturn false reasoning before he can plant the seeds of truth. It can also be earnestly contending for the faith and saving one from losing their faith, as they have begun to doubt. Moreover, it can involve rebuking those who contradict the truth. It is being prepared to make a defense to anyone who asks the Christian evangelist for a reason for the hope that is in him or her.–Jude 1.3, 21-23; 1 Pet 3.15; Acts 17:2-3; Titus 1:9.

What do we mean by **obligated** and what we mean by **evangelism** are at the heart of the matter and are indeed related to each other?

EVANGELISM: An evangelist is a proclaimer of the gospel or good news, as well as all biblical truths. There are levels of evangelism, which is pictured in first-century Christianity. All Christians evangelized in the first century, but a select few fit the role of a full-time evangelist (Ephesians 4:8, 11-12), as was true of Philip and Timothy.

Both Philip and Timothy are specifically mentioned as evangelizers. (Ac 21:8; 2 Tim. 4:5) Philip was a full-time evangelist after Pentecost, who was sent to the city of Samaria, having great success. An angel even directed Philip to an Ethiopian Eunuch, to share the good news about Christ with him. Because of the Eunuch's already having knowledge of God by way of the Old Testament, Philip was able to help him understand that the Hebrew Scriptures pointed to Christ as the long awaited Messiah. In the end, Philip baptized the Eunuch. After that, the Spirit again sent Philip on a mission, this time to Azotus and all the cities on the way to Caesarea. (Ac 8:5, 12, 14, 26-40) Paul evangelized in many lands, setting up one congregation after another. (2 Cor. 10:13-16) Timothy was an evangelizer or missionary, and Paul placed distinct importance on evangelizing when he gave his parting encouragement to Timothy.–2 Timothy 4:5; 1 Timothy 1:3.

The office of apostle and evangelist seem to overlap in some areas, but could be distinguished in that apostles traveled and set up congregations, which took evangelizing skills, but also developed the congregations after they were established. The evangelists were more of a missionary, being stationed in certain areas to grow and develop congregations. In addition, if we look at all of the apostles and the evangelists, plus Paul's more than one hundred traveling companions, it seems very unlikely that they could have had Christianity at over one million by the 125 C.E. This was accomplished because all Christians were obligated to carry out some level of evangelism.

OBLIGATED: In the broadest sense of the term for evangelizer, all Christians are obligated to play some role as an evangelist.

• *Basic Evangelism* is planting seeds of truth and watering any seeds that have been planted. [In the basic sense of this word (euaggelistes), this would involve all Christians.] In some cases, it may be that one Christian planted the seed, which was initially rejected, so he was left in a good way because the planter did not try to force the truth down his throat. However, later he faces something in life that moves him to reconsider those seeds and another

Christian waters what had already been planted by the first Christian. This evangelism can be carried out in all of the methods that are available: informal, house-to-house, street, phone, the internet, and the like. What amount of time is invested in the evangelism work is up to each Christian to decide for themselves?

• *Making Disciples* is having any role in the process of getting an unbeliever from his unbelief state to the point of accepting Christ as his Savior and being baptized. Once the unbeliever has become a believer, he is still developed until he has become strong. Any Christian could potentially carry this one person through all of the developmental stages. On the other hand, it may be that several have some part. It is like a person that specializes in a certain aspect of a job, but all are aware of the other aspects, in case they are called on to carry out that phase. Again, each Christian must decide for themselves what role they are to have, and how much of a role, but should be prepared to fill any role if needed.

• *Part-Time or Full-Time Evangelist* is one who sees this as their calling and chooses to be very involved as an evangelist in their local church and community. They may work part-time to supplement their work as an evangelist. They may be married with children, but they realize their gift is in the field of evangelism. If it were the wife, the husband would work toward supporting her work as an evangelist and vice-versa. If it were a single person, he or she would supplement their work by being employed part-time, but also the church would help as well. This person is well trained in every aspect of bringing one to Christ.

• *Congregation Evangelists* should be very involved in evangelizing their communities and helping the church members play their role at the basic levels of evangelism. There is nothing to say that one church could not have many within, who take on part-time or full-time evangelism within the congregation, which would and should be cultivated.[25]

The Identifying Mark of a Godly One

The marks of a true Christian would be like the different lines that make up a person's fingerprint, a print that **cannot** belong to any other person. The true Christians contain their own unique grouping of marks, forming a positive "fingerprint" that **cannot** belong to any other person.

Are we sure that we are truly walking in the truth? What kind of self-examination is fitting for servants of God? The Apostle Paul exhorted the Christians at Corinth to "**examine yourselves**, to see whether you are in the faith. **Test yourselves**." (2 Cor. 13:5) Why should Paul's admonition to the Corinthians be of interest to us? We can do the same today. It will protect us from being uncertain as to whether we are walking in the truth. What standard do we have for testing whether we are in the faith, and why is that the perfect standard? If we are going to take a test to see whether we are truly in the faith, namely, truly walking with God, we must measure our conduct in light of the Word of God.

William Lange Craig wrote, "Remember that our faith is not based on emotions, but on the truth, and therefore you must hold on to it." What truth? Jesus said to the Father in prayer, "Sanctify them in the truth; your word is truth ." (John 17:17) By identifying the Scriptures some of which

---

actually say, "**You are my disciples if …,**" we can know if we are truly Christian. A test that can actually tell us whether we are walking in the truth should never be based on emotionalism, but rather on Scripture. Do our words, our thoughts, our actions, our mind, our heart attitude harmonize with the Scriptures? Within this publication, we will be able to let the Word of God **prove** who we really are. Let us follow the Apostle Paul's counsel, by testing ourselves to determine whether we are adhering to God's Word.

The book **EVIDENCE THAT YOU ARE TRULY CHRISTIAN** uses the **BIBLE ALONE** to identify the marks of those who are TRULY CHRISTIAN. Paul commanded that we do this, so if we refuse to test ourselves against these Biblical markers is to disobey the inspired Word of God. Paul commanded that we **EXAMINE OURSELVES.**[26]

---

[26] https://www.christianpublishers.org/webstore

CHAPTER 7 In Union with Love

The Need for Avoiding Preconceptions and Biases

To achieve true enlightenment of Bible truth, it's essential to avoid preconceptions, biases, and assumptions that are not rooted in Scripture. When we come to the text with a pre-formed understanding or opinions that align more with cultural norms or religious traditions than with what the Scripture actually says, we risk misinterpreting God's Word. It's crucial to remain objective and approach the Bible using the Historical-Grammatical method of interpretation. This ensures that the text is understood in its original context, making room for an accurate understanding of God's will and character.

John 3:16 as the Fullest Expression of God's Love

When considering what the Scriptures set forth as the fullest expression of God's love, the verse that immediately comes to mind is John 3:16: "For God so loved the world that he gave his only begotten Son, in order that whoever believes in him will not be destroyed but have eternal life." This single verse captures the essence of divine love, demonstrating God's willingness to sacrifice for the good of humanity.

The Centrality of Divine Love

Understanding this expression of God's love is central to grasping the truth that "God is love" (1 John 4:8, 16). His love is not mere sentiment but is action-oriented, focused on the best interest of those He loves. God's love manifested in giving His only begotten Son is the epitome of selfless sacrifice, the ultimate demonstration of love. Romans 5:8 reinforces this by stating, "But God shows his love for us in that while we were still sinners, Christ died for us."

Aligning Ourselves with God's Love

The more we understand and meditate on this profound expression of God's love, the more we will find ourselves aligned with it. This is not a mere intellectual exercise but a transformative experience that molds our character and actions. 1 John 4:19 tells us, "We love because he first loved us," implying that understanding God's love empowers us to love others more effectively. This alignment brings us closer to God, facilitating a deepening union with divine love. The apostle Paul prayed for this very experience for the Ephesian believers: "And to know the love of Christ which surpasses knowledge, that you may be filled up to all the fullness of God" (Ephesians 3:19).

The Ultimate Goal: Union with Divine Love

As we continually align ourselves more and more with God's expression of love, we can anticipate an ever-deepening union with divine love. This is the ultimate goal for any Christian seeking to grow in faith and spiritual maturity. Through the experience of understanding, living, and sharing God's love, we not only grow in our relationship with Him but also reflect His character to the world around us. This union with divine love is the ultimate realization of the Christian hope and the very essence of eternal life, as stated in John 17:3: "And this is eternal life, that they may know you, the only true God, and Jesus Christ whom you have sent."

Understanding "The World" in John 3:16

In the context of John 3:16, "For God so loved the world," the term "the world" (Greek: *kosmos*) is often subject to various interpretations. However, in this specific context, "the world" signifies all of humanity—every individual from every tribe, tongue, and nation. This is made explicit by the universality of the offer that follows: "that whoever believes in Him will not be destroyed but have eternal life."

In other words, God's love isn't limited to a specific group of people or a particular ethnicity or culture. His love encompasses all humans irrespective of their background. This understanding is crucial in maintaining the universality of the Gospel message, underlined further in verses like 1 Timothy 2:4, which states that God "desires all men to be saved and to come to the knowledge of the truth."

Misunderstandings of "The World" in Christian Circles

Unfortunately, the term "the world" is often misunderstood in various Christian circles, leading to different kinds of theological errors. Here are some common misunderstandings:

1. **Exclusivity**: Some factions within Christianity have interpreted "the world" to mean only those who are predestined to be saved, limiting God's love to a select group. This view is at odds with the universality expressed in the Scriptures.

2. **Universalism**: On the other end of the spectrum is the view that "the world" means everyone will ultimately be saved, negating the conditional "whoever believes in Him" in the same verse. This contradicts other biblical passages that clearly articulate that not everyone will receive eternal life (e.g., Matthew 7:21-23, Revelation 20:15).

3. **Moral Indifference**: Another misunderstanding is that God's love for "the world" implies that He is morally indifferent to human sin. This is refuted by passages like Romans 6:23, which states, "For the wages of sin is death, but the free gift of God is eternal life in Christ Jesus our Lord."

4. **Cultural Conformance**: Some Christians mistake "loving the world" as an endorsement to embrace worldly culture and systems, overlooking the biblical warning against loving the world in the sense of its sinful patterns (1 John 2:15-17).

Significance of Correctly Understanding "The World"

The correct understanding of "the world" in John 3:16 has profound implications for evangelism, theology, and Christian living. It helps us grasp the broad scope of God's love, while also understanding the condition of belief required for eternal life. By getting this right, we align ourselves more closely with the truth of Scripture and God's character, ensuring that our evangelistic efforts and theological constructs are biblically sound.

Clarification: 'The World' as 'The World of Redeemable Humankind'

The phrase "the world" in John 3:16 should be more precisely understood as "the world of redeemable humankind." This means that while God's love extends to all people in a general sense, the specific salvific benefits of that love are available only to those who accept Jesus Christ as their Savior and undergo a transformative spiritual rebirth, often referred to as being "born again" (John 3:3-8).

The Necessity of Change and Transformation

It's crucial to emphasize that coming to Christ requires change. Paul speaks of this transformation as becoming a "new creation" (2 Corinthians 5:17). This change is not superficial; it involves a turning away from sin and a turning toward God—a concept Scripturally known as repentance (Acts 3:19). Believers must move from their old selves, characterized by sinful behaviors, to their new selves, characterized by godliness and holiness (Ephesians 4:22-24).

Limitations of the Ransom Sacrifice Regarding Unrepentant Sin

The ransom sacrifice of Jesus Christ is indeed sufficient to remove the stain of Adamic sin, to forgive past sins, and to offer grace for occasional lapses into sin. However, it's imperative to understand that this sacrifice does not extend its benefits to unrepentant, ongoing practice of sin. The Apostle John makes this clear when he states that no one who abides in Christ "keeps on sinning" (1 John 3:6). The continuous, unrepentant practice of sin puts one in a precarious spiritual state, endangering their prospects for eternal life (Hebrews 10:26-27).

In summary, the term "the world" in John 3:16 should be understood as encompassing all of redeemable humankind. However, redemption and eternal life are conditional upon faith in Jesus Christ, repentance, and a resultant transformation of life. Without these, the individual remains outside the salvific love that God has extended through His Son.

Establishing the Context: The Logos in John 1:1-13

To grasp the depth of John 3:16, it is helpful to examine John 1:1-13 where the Apostle John introduces the concept of the *Logos*, or the Word, which is Jesus Christ. In this passage, the eternal nature of Christ as the *Logos* is emphasized ("In the beginning was the Word, and the Word was with God, and the Word was God" - John 1:1). We also find that the *Logos* is instrumental in the creation of the world ("All things were made through him, and without him was not any thing made that was made" - John 1:3).

The Incarnation: The Word Becomes Flesh

One of the major points in John 1 is the Incarnation, where the *Logos* becomes flesh and dwells among us (John 1:14). This is crucial because it sets the stage for the redemptive work that the *Logos* will undertake, which is the focal point of John 3:16.

The Rejection and Acceptance of the Light

John 1:10-13 further highlights that the world did not recognize or accept the *Logos* ("He was in the world, and the world was made through him, yet the world did not know him" - John 1:10). However, to those who did accept Him, the *Logos* gave the right to become children of God (John 1:12).

Tying it to John 3:16: The Ultimate Act of God's Love through the Logos

When we come to John 3:16, we understand that the gift of God's "only begotten Son" is none other than this *Logos*, who was with God in the beginning, through whom the world was made, and who became flesh to dwell among us. The act of giving His Son for the world's redemption is, therefore, an act of unimaginable love, not just because of the sacrifice involved, but because of who the Son is—He is the *Logos*, part of the Godhead, through whom the world was made.

The Fullest Expression of God's Love: In Union with the Logos

Therefore, the fullest expression of God's love, as you've noted in your article "In Union with Love: Based on John 3:16," is found in His giving of the *Logos* for the world's redemption. Understanding the identity and role of the *Logos* from John 1:1-13 enriches our comprehension of the magnitude of God's love expressed in John 3:16. By aligning ourselves with this ultimate expression of divine love—by believing in the Son—we are not just beneficiaries of God's love but become children of God (John 1:12), entering into a union with divine love itself.

The Profound Implications of Divine Love: A Call for Transformational Response

The theological and soteriological dimensions of God's love, as expounded in your article "In Union with Love: Based on John 3:16," necessitate an earnest and transformative response from believers. The monumental revelation that God so loved the world to give His only begotten Son requires more than mere intellectual assent; it demands a transformative life journey.

Faith in the Only Begotten Son

The initial response called forth is faith in Jesus Christ, the *Logos* and the only begotten Son of God (John 3:16). This faith is not just acknowledging facts about Christ but involves trusting Him for salvation. Faith is the mechanism that activates God's promise of eternal life (Ephesians 2:8-9).

Repentance and Spiritual Rebirth

Beyond mere belief, this faith should inspire repentance. True repentance is a change of mind about sin and God, resulting in a change of life direction. This echoes Jesus' words that one must be "born again" to see the Kingdom of God (John 3:3). This spiritual rebirth is not merely symbolic; it signifies a real, profound change in the believer's life.

A Life of Obedience and Sanctification

Once one is justified by faith, the journey doesn't end; it begins anew in sanctification. It's crucial to stress that faith without works is dead (James 2:17). A life committed to Christ will naturally produce good works, not as a basis for salvation, but as an evidence of a changed heart. The Apostle Paul emphasized the importance of walking in the Spirit to not gratify the desires of the flesh (Galatians 5:16).

Cultivation of Christian Virtues

As faith develops, so should Christian virtues. Peter, in his second epistle, lists these virtues as a sequential outgrowth of faith: virtue, knowledge, self-control, perseverance, godliness, brotherly kindness, and love (2 Peter 1:5-7). These virtues aren't optional add-ons to a Christian's life but rather should be the identifying features of someone transformed by God's love.

Brotherly Love and Evangelism

Moreover, an understanding and appreciation of God's love should inevitably lead us to love our brothers and sisters (1 John 4:11). Not only that, but it should also fuel a commitment to evangelism, urging us to share the good news of God's love with the world (Matthew 28:19-20).

Perseverance in Righteousness

Given the eternally consequential nature of God's love, as you have also emphasized, one must persist in the faith, steering clear from the unrepentant practice of sin. Hebrews 10:26-27 offers a stern warning to those who deliberately keep on sinning after having received the knowledge of the truth.

In Summary: A Multi-Faceted, Life-Long Response

In conclusion, God's love isn't just a theological concept to be admired but a transformative power to be experienced and responded to. This response should be multi-faceted, involving faith, repentance, sanctification, the cultivation of virtues, love for others, and unyielding perseverance. Only then can one confidently look forward to being eternally in union with divine love.

CHAPTER 8 The Greatest of These Is Love

The Paramount Importance of Love: A Faith-Rooted, Hope-Driven Obligation to Love

In accordance with your focus on 1 Corinthians 13:13 within your article, "The Greatest of These Is Love," the text functions as a theological and ethical crescendo in Pauline thought. It encapsulates the essence of what Christian life should be: faith, hope, and love. However, Paul is meticulous in emphasizing that the greatest of these is love.

The Triad of Virtues: Faith, Hope, and Love

Before delving into love specifically, it's crucial to appreciate the triad Paul presents. Faith, hope, and love are essential to Christian living. Faith is the foundation of our relationship with God, enabled by His grace (Ephesians 2:8-9). Hope is what fuels our perseverance, the eager anticipation of eternal life with God (Romans 8:24-25). Both faith and hope are integral, but they are incomplete without love.

Love as the Pinnacle of Christian Virtue

Paul underscores that *the greatest of these is love*. It's not that faith and hope are unimportant; rather, they find their highest expression and fulfillment in love. Galatians 5:6 even states that the only thing that counts is "*faith expressing itself through love*."

Love's Manifestation in Relational Ethics

The call to love isn't limited to an emotional or passive disposition but manifests in action. In the broader context of 1 Corinthians 13, love is patient, kind, not envious, not boastful, not arrogant, and so forth. These are not merely internal attitudes but relational ethics affecting how we treat God and our neighbor (Matthew 22:36-40).

Love as a Reflection of God's Own Character

We are called to love because God Himself is love (1 John 4:8). Our capability to love is derived from God's love for us, as manifest supremely in the gift of His Son (John 3:16). The Apostle John sums it up well when he says that we love because He first loved us (1 John 4:19).

Love's Imperative in Evangelism and Discipleship

If we have genuinely experienced God's transformative love, it should be our compulsion to share this with others. Love should be the motivating factor in evangelism (Matthew 28:18-20) and discipleship (John 13:34-35).

Love as the Ultimate Measure of Spiritual Maturity

The Christian walk is not merely about doctrinal accuracy or ritualistic purity but spiritual maturity manifest in love. The ultimate test of our spiritual development is not how much we know but how much we love (1 John 3:14-18).

The Unfading Nature of Love

Interestingly, love is the only element in the triad that will continue in the age to come. Faith will be made sight; hope will be realized, but love will endure forever. The Apostle Peter says that love covers a multitude of sins (1 Peter 4:8), suggesting its enduring and transformative power.

An All-Consuming, Ongoing Commitment to Love

To sum up, the immense love of God should elicit from us an all-consuming love—for God and our neighbors. It should be the defining characteristic of our lives, guiding our actions, attitudes, and ambitions. Love is not merely one virtue among many but the very essence and culmination of Christian existence.

The Biblical Depictions of Romantic Love: A Canonical Exploration

When we explore the notion of romantic love within the parameters of biblical text, it's essential to recognize that romantic love, in its appropriate context, is considered both honorable and beautiful. The concept of romantic love isn't relegated to the secular or profane but finds representation in several Scriptural accounts. Below are key examples.

Adam and Eve: The Primordial Romance

The narrative in Genesis 2 presents the first marital union as a profound act of divine orchestration. When Adam sees Eve for the first time, his poetic exclamation, "*This at last is bone of my bones and flesh of my flesh*" (Genesis 2:23), conveys more than a sense of relief; it signifies the divine institution of marital love. In this first couple, we see a form of romantic love that was designed to be complementary and purposeful.

Isaac and Rebekah: Love Grows in Covenant

The account of Isaac and Rebekah in Genesis 24 serves as an example of love within arranged marriages in biblical times. Isaac loved Rebekah (Genesis 24:67), and the description implies a deep affection that was more than mere infatuation. The commitment and fidelity seen in their relationship underscore the importance of enduring love within the marital covenant.

Edward D. Andrews

Jacob and Rachel: Love Worth Waiting For

The story of Jacob and Rachel is a poignant example of romantic love. Jacob serves seven years to earn Rachel's hand, and they seem to him but a few days "because of his love for her" (Genesis 29:20). Though their story had its complications—due to Laban's trickery leading Jacob to marry Leah first—the love he had for Rachel is clear.

Song of Solomon: The Poetry of Passionate Love

The Song of Solomon is perhaps the most overt expression of romantic love in the Bible. It is a poetic narrative that explores the emotional, physical, and even the erotic dimensions of love between a husband and wife. Phrases like "*Let him kiss me with the kisses of his mouth! For your love is better than wine*" (Song of Solomon 1:2), emphasize the passionate aspect of romantic love within the sanctity of marriage.

Hosea and Gomer: Redeeming Love

The prophet Hosea's marriage to Gomer may not initially appear as a romantic tale given her infidelity. However, Hosea's persistent love for his unfaithful wife serves as a vivid portrayal of God's redeeming love for His people. Hosea's love transcends the romantic and moves into the realm of sacrificial, reflecting the greater love of God (Hosea 3:1).

Boaz and Ruth: A Love Story of Redemption and Kindness

The story of Ruth and Boaz serves as another example. Here, romantic love is coupled with redemption and characterized by mutual respect and kindness. Boaz's actions toward Ruth are noble and protective, while Ruth's loyalty to Naomi and her budding love for Boaz showcase love's multifaceted dimensions (Ruth 3:9-11).

Mary and Joseph: A Love Born of Divine Purpose

Though not elaborated upon extensively, the relationship between Mary and Joseph in the New Testament demonstrates a form of romantic love that was committed, enduring, and grounded in faithfulness to God and each other (Matthew 1:19-25).

The Sanctity and Diversity of Romantic Love in Scripture

Romantic love, as depicted in these biblical narratives, is honorable, varied, and deeply human. While the ultimate form of love—agape love—is underscored in texts like 1 Corinthians 13:13 as the greatest virtue, these examples remind us that romantic love, in its rightful context, is a divine gift to be cherished and upheld.

The Manifestation of Family Love in Biblical Texts: A Comprehensive Analysis

Family love stands as a foundational component of human society, and it's no surprise that the Scriptures offer an array of examples that vividly illustrate the various dimensions of familial love. In many ways, these instances can be seen as a reflection of divine love, although they operate within the limitations of human nature. Let's explore some of the most notable examples.

Parental Love: Abraham and Isaac

The story of Abraham and Isaac in Genesis 22 epitomizes the profound love and trust that can exist between parent and child. Abraham's willingness to sacrifice Isaac at God's command exemplifies an ultimate act of faith in God, but it also underscores the gravity of his love for his son. The account reveals that family love, while immensely powerful, should be subordinate to love for God. Conversely, Isaac's trust in his father, even when bound for sacrifice, shows the ideal of a child's love and respect for a parent.

Sibling Love: Jonathan and David

The love between Jonathan, the son of King Saul, and David is one of the most iconic examples of fraternal love in the Bible. Although not biological brothers, their love is often taken as an archetype for sibling love. Jonathan's protection of David from Saul's murderous intentions shows a form of love that is selfless and courageous (1 Samuel 18:1-3, 20:17).

Brotherly Responsibility: Joseph and His Brothers

Joseph's experience with his brothers is filled with ups and downs, to say the least. Initially, jealousy and rivalry lead his brothers to sell him into slavery (Genesis 37). However, the eventual reconciliation between Joseph and his brothers (Genesis 45) illustrates the transformative power of familial love, forgiveness, and redemption.

Marital Love: Adam and Eve

As mentioned before, the love between Adam and Eve establishes the basic building block for all future families. Their union, presented as "one flesh" in Genesis 2:24, emphasizes the close, inseparable nature of marital love. While their story includes moments of failure and blame (Genesis 3), it also shows a partnership that endures challenges and consequences.

The Dutiful Child: Jesus and His Earthly Parents

The Gospel accounts provide a glimpse into Jesus' relationship with his earthly parents, Mary and Joseph. His submission to them after being found in the Temple is an indication of his respect and love for his parents (Luke 2:51). In this, we find a model for the kind of love and obedience that children ought to offer to their parents.

The Prodigal Son: A Lesson in Unconditional Love

The parable of the Prodigal Son in Luke 15:11-32 gives us a vivid picture of unconditional familial love. The father's love in the parable mirrors God's love for humanity but also serves as an example for earthly parents. The father's joyful acceptance of his wayward son stands as a testament to the enduring, forgiving nature of parental love.

Spousal Love: The Love Chapter

While not directly aimed at familial love, the principles in 1 Corinthians 13 can be applied within the family framework. Patience, kindness, and perseverance are as essential in familial relationships as they are in romantic or platonic ones. In a way, 1 Corinthians 13:13 serves as a general principle that could be extended to familial love: **"But now faith, hope, love, abide these three; but the greatest of these is love."**

The Multifaceted Nature of Family Love in Scripture

The Bible doesn't present an idealized picture of family love; rather, it shows love operating in the midst of human imperfections and complexities. These Scriptural accounts challenge us to bring the principle of 1 Corinthians 13:13 into our familial relationships, to love in both word and deed, in patience and kindness, ever striving for the ideal that the greatest of these is indeed love.

Lack of Natural Affection in Contemporary Times: A Biblical Assessment

The concept of natural affection is deeply rooted in the Bible, encapsulating the kinds of familial and community bonds that God intends for human relationships. The Bible is unequivocal in stating that love, the highest of virtues, should guide these interactions (1 Corinthians 13:13). However, we observe a considerable shift away from this ideal in our current era. Here are some areas where this is manifest:

Breakdown of Family Units

The family, designed to be a cornerstone of societal stability and a cradle of love, is increasingly under threat. Divorce rates have surged, and parent-child relationships are often strained. In many instances, children are disobedient to parents, and parents are disengaged from their God-given role to nurture their offspring (2 Timothy 3:1-2). The dissolution of the family unit signifies a direct contravention of God's design for human relationships to be driven by love and natural affection.

Increasing Isolation and Self-Centeredness

With the rise of social media and an increasingly interconnected world, one would assume that people are more connected than ever. Paradoxically, the opposite is often true. Many people report feeling isolated and lonely, indicating a breakdown in community life that should ideally be characterized by natural affection and mutual support (Hebrews 10:24-25).

Erosion of Empathy

There's a noticeable erosion of empathy in interactions between people, whether on social media platforms, political discourses, or even day-to-day communications. In contrast, the Bible encourages believers to "rejoice with those who rejoice, weep with those who weep" (Romans 12:15).

Violent and Harmful Behavior

The rise in violent crimes, cyberbullying, and general apathy toward human suffering further exemplify the lack of natural affection in contemporary society. Scriptures strongly condemn such attitudes. Proverbs 6:16-19 mentions "hands that shed innocent blood" and "a heart that devises wicked plans" among the things that are detestable to God.

Disintegration of Community Support Systems

Traditional community support systems that existed to help the vulnerable—such as the elderly, orphans, and widows—are disintegrating. This disintegration contravenes Scriptural injunctions that call for the care of those who are less fortunate (James 1:27).

An Escalation in False Forms of Love

The modern concept of love is often distorted, sometimes equated with lust or seen as transactional. This stands in stark contrast to the agape love described in the Bible, which is selfless and seeks the good of the other (1 Corinthians 13:4-7).

A Crisis of Love in Modern Times

The absence of natural affection in these and other areas highlights a significant spiritual crisis. The erosion of love in its purest, most divine form leaves society fragmented and individuals isolated. Returning to the biblical foundation that emphasizes love as the greatest of virtues (1 Corinthians 13:13) provides not just an alternative but a solution to the societal maladies plaguing contemporary life.

Affection Between Friends in the Bible: An In-Depth Analysis

Friendship is another form of relationship wherein love plays a central role. The Bible offers us numerous examples of deep affection and love between friends, and these examples often serve as models for the kind of friendships that believers should aspire to have. While not as emphasized as familial or marital relationships, friendships are nonetheless significant and can be guided by the principle found in 1 Corinthians 13:13. Let's delve into some of the most remarkable instances.

David and Jonathan: The Archetype of Biblical Friendship

The friendship between David and Jonathan, son of King Saul, remains one of the most compelling illustrations of deep affection and loyalty between friends. We read in 1 Samuel 18:1, "As soon as he had finished speaking to Saul, the soul of Jonathan was knit to the soul of David, and Jonathan loved him as his own soul." Jonathan's commitment to David goes beyond mere companionship;

he willingly risks his life and position for David's safety (1 Samuel 20:1-42). This friendship is often seen as the gold standard of what a biblical friendship rooted in love should look like.

Ruth and Naomi: Devotion Beyond Law

While the relationship between Ruth and Naomi is technically one of in-laws, their bond transitions into one that can only be described as deep friendship. Ruth's famous words to Naomi, "Where you go I will go, and where you stay I will stay. Your people will be my people and your God my God" (Ruth 1:16), epitomize the kind of love and loyalty that should characterize friendships. Their story is a testament to the kind of commitment and affection that can exist between friends, almost akin to family.

Paul and Timothy: Mentorship Rooted in Love

The New Testament presents the relationship between the Apostle Paul and Timothy as another strong example of affection between friends. Although Paul is in many ways a mentor to Timothy, the mutual affection they share is evident. Paul refers to Timothy as his "beloved and faithful child in the Lord" (1 Corinthians 4:17). The emotional depth of their relationship is also evident when Paul says, "I have no one else of kindred spirit who will genuinely be concerned for your welfare" (Philippians 2:20).

Jesus and Lazarus: Affection Transcending Death

The Gospel of John records the friendship between Jesus and Lazarus, along with his sisters Martha and Mary. Jesus' love for this family is evident, but his friendship with

Lazarus is specially highlighted when Lazarus dies. Jesus wept at the news of his friend's death (John 11:35), and His subsequent raising of Lazarus from the dead serves as a powerful testament to the depth of affection He had for his friend.

Barnabas: The Encourager

Although less highlighted, the friendship between Paul and Barnabas deserves mention. Barnabas is often called the 'Son of Encouragement,' and his relationship with Paul demonstrates this well. They engage in missionary journeys together and even though they eventually part ways over a disagreement, the initial years reveal a friendship based on mutual respect and a shared vision (Acts 13:2, 15:36-41).

Friendship as a Reflection of Divine Love

While friendship may not always be the central focus of biblical narratives, these examples offer us significant insights into how affection and love should operate within the realm of friendships. These relationships often mirror the qualities outlined in the "love chapter" of 1 Corinthians 13, which concludes that "the greatest of these is love." In friendships, just as in familial and romantic relationships, love remains the highest virtue to be cultivated and cherished.

The Nature and Manifestation of Agape Love

The term "agape" resonates profoundly in the New Testament as the epitome of the kind of love that should be the guiding principle in Christian life. To fully grasp the nature and implications of this form of love, it is important to consult the Biblical text exhaustively.

The Semantics of Agape

In the New Testament, particularly in Pauline theology, the Greek term used for love at its pinnacle is "agape." This term appears in 1 Corinthians 13:13, an oft-cited verse that emphasizes love as the greatest virtue, superior even to faith and hope. Agape is not merely an affectionate feeling; it is an act of the will. This is a love guided or governed by principle, concerned with doing good to others regardless of their merits or any benefits that may accrue to the giver.

Agape: The Love That Is God Himself

Agape love is so central to the Christian understanding of God that the apostle John declares, "God is love" (1 John 4:8, 16). This statement reflects the nature of God's character, revealing that He not only shows love but is the embodiment of it. This love is perfectly demonstrated in His willingness to sacrifice His only-begotten Son for the redemption of humanity (John 3:16).

The Cost of Agape

Agape love is sacrificial. Paul vividly describes this when he says, "For one will scarcely die for a righteous man, though perhaps for a good man one would dare even to die. But God shows his love for us in that while we were still sinners, Christ died for us" (Romans 5:7-8). The immense cost of this love is that it is given freely, even when it requires the ultimate sacrifice.

The Universality of Agape

Agape love is indiscriminate and universal. It doesn't discriminate based on social status, ethnicity, or any other human category. It is a love that even extends to one's enemies (Matthew 5:44). It does good to others regardless of their status in life, and its blessings are poured out even on those who may not reciprocate the love or deserve it on moral or ethical grounds.

Agape in Daily Life

While the ultimate example of agape love is seen in the sacrifice of Christ, its practical application should be evident in the lives of believers. Whether in serving the needy (James 1:27), forgiving others (Ephesians 4:32), or in day-to-day interactions with people (Colossians 3:12-14), this love should be the mark of a genuine Christian life.

Agape as the Guiding Principle

The essence of agape love transcends human limitations and frailties, touching the divine. Its preeminence, as stated in 1 Corinthians 13:13, should not be understood merely as a hierarchy of virtues but as the core principle that informs and transcends all virtues. It is a transformative force, capable of changing not only the individual but also the world at large. In practicing agape, we come closer to the divine love that God has shown to humanity, making it the ultimate goal of the Christian life.

The Supremacy of Agape Over Faith

The New Testament text unequivocally places agape love at the pinnacle of virtues, even above faith. This notion prompts us to inquire: Why is agape greater than faith? To answer this, we delve deeply into Paul's theological framework, primarily utilizing his guidance in 1 Corinthians 13:2 and comparing this with other biblical texts.

Agape as the Fundamental Essence

First, it is crucial to understand that Paul is not demeaning or diminishing the value of faith. Faith is essential for salvation, as affirmed by Ephesians 2:8: "For by grace you have been saved through faith." Rather, Paul is emphasizing that agape love is the most excellent way to manifest faith in God. Love is the essence of God's character (1 John 4:8), and thereby, it should also be the defining quality of God's children.

The Limitation of Faith Without Love

Paul outlines an intriguing scenario in 1 Corinthians 13:2: "And if I have the gift of prophecy, and understand all mysteries and all knowledge, and if I have all faith, so as to remove mountains, but have not love, I am nothing." The phrase "I am nothing" is extremely telling. This indicates that faith, though capable of 'removing mountains' as alluded to in Matthew 17:20, is insufficient on its own.

The Danger of Selfish Faith

If faith is exercised without the underpinning of agape love, there is a risk of it serving selfish purposes. Such faith is devoid of the qualities that God esteems. Jesus himself warned that many will 'prophesy in his name, expel demons in his name, and perform many powerful works in his name,' but will not find His approval (Matthew 7:22-23). In these cases, faith and works are oriented towards self-glorification rather than God's glory and the well-being of others.

Agape: The Evidential Force of Genuine Faith

Agape love is the ultimate evidence of genuine faith. As James 2:17 puts it, "So also faith by itself, if it does not have works, is dead." These 'works' are not simply deeds but are the embodiments of agape love. When one's faith is deeply rooted in this form of love, it becomes vivified and effective, fulfilling its divine purpose.

The Timeless Nature of Agape

Another reason for the supremacy of agape over faith is its eternal continuity. Faith will find its consummation in sight when believers are in the presence of God, but love will continue eternally. This makes it the greatest since it aligns with the eternal nature of God Himself.

The Integral Relationship Between Faith and Agape

While faith is indispensable for a relationship with God and for salvation, it reaches its most elevated form when accompanied by agape love. In essence, faith needs agape to reach its fullest, most God-honoring potential. Without love, even the most profound faith turns hollow, failing to fulfill its divinely ordained function. Thus, agape stands as the greatest of virtues, for it not only validates faith but also unifies and completes all other godly traits.

The Superiority of Agape Over Hope

The theological triad of faith, hope, and love has been crucial in shaping Christian ethics and beliefs. However, Paul's insistence in 1 Corinthians 13:13 that "the greatest of these is love" raises pertinent questions regarding the relative weights of these virtues. It is critical to understand why agape love is considered superior to hope in biblical terms.

The Self-Centered Nature of Hope

One of the key differences between hope and agape love lies in their orientation. Hope can be inherently self-focused. That is, one hopes for a particular outcome that benefits oneself. This self-interest could range from personal salvation to temporal blessings. Hope, as powerful as it is for motivation and endurance, can sometimes be a means to fulfill individual desires or ambitions. In contrast, agape love "is not seeking its own interests" (1 Corinthians 13:4, 5). This love goes beyond self to consider and act for the wellbeing of others. It signifies an outward orientation, a giving rather than receiving.

The Transient Quality of Hope

Hope is a future-oriented virtue, rooted in the belief in a better tomorrow, whether that means personal prosperity, spiritual maturity, or eschatological fulfillment. However, hope finds its completion when its object is realized. For example, the hope for eternal life ceases to be hope when one actually enters into that life. As Paul mentions in Romans 8:24-25, "For in hope we were saved, but hope that is seen is not hope, for who hopes for what he sees? But if we hope for what we do not see, we eagerly wait for it with patience." Once hope is actualized, it has served its purpose and ceases to be a driving force.

The Eternal Continuity of Agape Love

In contrast, agape love has an enduring and eternal nature. Paul affirms that love "endures all things" and that it "never fails" (1 Corinthians 13:7, 8). While hope finds its culmination in the realization of what is hoped for, love continues to exist and operate. In the eternal state, when all hopes have been fulfilled, love will continue to characterize the interactions among the redeemed and between the redeemed and God.

The Comprehensive Scope of Agape

While hope is often tied to specific outcomes or circumstances, agape love has a much broader range. It is not limited by time, place, or situation but is applicable in all interactions and relationships. It is the love that causes God to act for our good, and it is the love that should drive us to act for the good of others.

The Completeness of Agape

Agape love is not just another virtue among many; it is the virtue that gives life and meaning to all other virtues, including hope. Hope might be the fuel that drives us forward, but love is the road itself, as well as the vehicle we use to travel. It is the enduring and eternal quality that reflects the very nature of God. Therefore, according to the Scriptural narrative, while faith, hope, and love are essential elements of the Christian life, agape love stands supreme, encapsulating and fulfilling the essence of what it means to be in a relationship with God and with others.

Love as the Greatest of God's Four Cardinal Attributes

When we examine God's nature as revealed in Scripture, we find a Being of infinite wisdom, justice, power, and love. However, a close scrutiny reveals that love stands preeminent among these cardinal attributes. Not only is this consistent with the apostolic teaching that "the greatest of these is love" (1 Corinthians 13:13), but it also aligns with the overarching message of Scripture concerning the nature of God.

Love as the Defining Characteristic of God

The Apostle John boldly declares, "God is love" (1 John 4:8, 16). This is a profound statement that encapsulates God's essence. It does not merely say that God possesses love but rather equates God with love. This is an exclusive statement; nowhere in the Scriptures do we find such a definitive assertion about God being wisdom, justice, or power. These are certainly attributes God possesses (Job

12:13; Psalm 147:5; Daniel 4:37), but they do not define Him in the way love does.

Love as the Motivating Force

All of God's actions and decisions emanate from His love. Whether it is the act of creation, the provision of salvation, or the execution of justice, love is the driving force. Jehovah's love is not an abstract quality; it manifests in concrete actions. John 3:16 epitomizes this by saying, "For God so loved the world, that he gave his only Son, that whoever believes in him should not perish but have eternal life." The giving of His Son is a monumental demonstration of love that sets the stage for all interactions between the divine and the human.

The Harmony and Balance of God's Attributes

It is essential to recognize that in Jehovah, these four attributes are not in tension but in perfect harmony. Love does not override wisdom, justice, or power; rather, it directs them. Wisdom allows God to devise perfect plans, justice ensures the righteousness of His actions, and power enables Him to accomplish His will. However, it is love that provides the moral and ethical framework within which these other attributes operate. Love is the lens through which God's wisdom, justice, and power are best understood.

The Relational Aspect of Love

Unlike wisdom, power, or justice, love inherently involves relationship and interaction. Whether it is God's love for humanity or the love between humans, it is a relational attribute. This aspect makes love the greatest attribute because the ultimate purpose of all creation and redemption is relational—to reconcile humanity to God and to one another.

The Primacy of Love

In summary, love is the greatest of God's attributes because it defines Him, motivates Him, and balances His other attributes. Love is the very essence of who God is and the reason for everything He does. This aligns perfectly with the Scriptural emphasis on love as the greatest virtue. Even God's wisdom, justice, and power are most fully understood and appreciated when viewed through the lens of His boundless love. Therefore, the statement that "the greatest of these is love" is not merely a comparison among human virtues but reflects a foundational truth about the nature of God Himself.

The Prime Motivator Behind Creation: Love, Not Wisdom or Power

The question of what motivated Jehovah to create the universe, as well as intelligent spirit and human beings, can be profoundly understood through the prism of God's attributes. While God possesses wisdom, power, and justice, it is essential to underline that love stands as the cornerstone of all His actions.

Love as the Creative Force

The Scripture says, "God is love" (1 John 4:8, 16). Notably, it does not say "God is power" or "God is wisdom." It is His love that drives Him to create. Love, by its very nature, seeks to share goodness, to expand the realm of well-being, to enrich others. Love involves relationship, the reaching out to 'the other,' and it finds its ultimate fulfillment in giving. This kind of unselfish love provides the motivation for creation. God's love was not content to remain within Himself but overflowed in the creation of a universe and beings capable of experiencing His love and reciprocating it.

Love Over Wisdom and Power

While it is true that God's wisdom is manifest in the intricate design of the universe and His power is evident in the sheer scale of creation, these are not the primary reasons He created. Wisdom and power serve as means, not ends. They are the tools used to accomplish a purpose, but they are not the purpose itself. Wisdom allows God to design the universe in a way that it operates harmoniously, and power enables Him to bring it into existence. But the desire to create in the first place springs from love.

Relational Aspects of Creation

The fact that God created intelligent spirit and human creatures adds weight to the argument that love is the prime motivator. Intelligence allows for the possibility of a relationship. God did not create automatons incapable of love but beings with free will who could choose to love Him in return. The kind of love God has is not a one-way street; it aims for a relationship, a two-way love that also seeks response. This corresponds well with the declaration in Genesis that humans are created in the image of God (Genesis 1:27), which includes the capacity to love.

God's motivation for creating the universe and intelligent beings was not rooted in a mere display of wisdom or an exhibition of power. Those attributes, although infinitely present in God, are secondary to love in the context of creation. Love is the purpose; wisdom and power are the means. Understanding this helps us appreciate more deeply the character of God and His relationship with His creation, and it further substantiates the apostolic statement that "the greatest of these is love" (1 Corinthians 13:13).

The Preeminence of Love Among the Fruits of the Spirit

The fruits of the Spirit are enumerated by the Apostle Paul in Galatians 5:22-23, where he states: "But the fruit of the Spirit is love, joy, peace, patience, kindness, goodness, faithfulness, gentleness, self-control." It is telling that the first quality he lists is love. While all these attributes are significant and complementary, love is given a distinct position at the forefront.

The Primacy of Love in the List

The listing of love as the first among the fruits of the Spirit is not incidental. Paul's ordering serves as a rhetorical tool to underscore love's centrality. By introducing love first, it sets the tone for all the other virtues, effectively framing them as different facets or expressions of love. For example, patience can be considered an expression of love toward those who are difficult to deal with, and kindness can be viewed as love in action.

The Indispensability of Love

The Apostle Paul stresses that love is not just another fruit of the Spirit; it is the essential one. In 1 Corinthians 13, sometimes called the "Love Chapter," Paul goes as far as to say that if one possesses various gifts or even great faith but lacks love, those qualities amount to nothing (1 Corinthians 13:2). This reflects the foundational text where Paul highlights that "the greatest of these is love" (1 Corinthians 13:13). If love is lacking, all other spiritual fruits lose their meaning and effectiveness.

Love as the Unifying Force

Love serves as the unifying thread that binds all the other fruits of the Spirit. The remaining fruits could be viewed as branches stemming from the trunk of love. Colossians 3:14 articulates this well, saying, "Above all these things put on love, which is the bond of perfection." Love acts as the glue that holds all virtues together, amplifying their impact and ensuring their genuineness.

Love holds a preeminent position among the fruits of the Spirit, not just because it is listed first but because of its indispensability and its unifying role among all other spiritual virtues. Understanding this aspect of love enriches the believer's understanding of the entire gamut of Christian virtues, confirming yet again why Paul emphasized that "the greatest of these is love."

Outstanding Fruits of Agape Love

Agape love, the highest form of love and the one that most closely aligns with God's nature, yields a variety of noteworthy fruits that impact both the individual and the community. These fruits serve as distinguishing marks of a life governed by divine love.

Self-Sacrifice

One of the most pronounced fruits of agape love is self-sacrifice. This goes beyond mere altruism; it's a willing, even joyful, setting aside of one's own desires and needs for the benefit of others. The epitome of this is Christ's sacrifice on the cross. As stated in John 15:13, "Greater love has no one than this, that someone lay down his life for his friends."

Humility

Agape love begets a humble spirit. This is not a self-degrading form of humility but one that esteems others better than oneself. Paul speaks to this when he writes, "Do nothing from selfish ambition or conceit, but in humility count others more significant than yourselves" (Philippians 2:3).

Forgiveness

Forgiveness is another consequential fruit of agape love. It reflects God's own forgiving nature, as described in Ephesians 4:32, "Be kind to one another, tender-hearted, forgiving one another, as God in Christ forgave you."

Kindness and Compassion

Acts of kindness and compassion are natural extensions of agape love. Even simple acts, like giving a cup of cold water to someone in need, are seen as significant in the eyes of God (Matthew 10:42).

Generosity

A generous spirit is yet another hallmark of agape love. This generosity isn't limited to material resources but extends to giving time, attention, and emotional support to others. Paul advises believers to excel in the grace of giving (2 Corinthians 8:7).

Patience and Endurance

The fruit of patience that comes from agape love is not passive but is a form of active endurance. It is the kind of patience that can endure hardship and continue to exhibit love and kindness despite difficult circumstances. It is the love that "endures all things" (1 Corinthians 13:7).

Peace and Harmony

Agape love fosters peace and harmony within communities. This is the peace that surpasses all understanding and has the power to unify diverse groups of people. Paul encourages the Colossians to "let the peace of Christ rule in your hearts" and to "be thankful" (Colossians 3:15).

Joy

Joy is a natural byproduct of agape love. Unlike mere happiness, which is fleeting and dependent on circumstances, this joy is deep-rooted and enduring. The joy that springs from agape love is highlighted by Jesus in John

15:11: "These things I have spoken to you, that my joy may be in you, and that your joy may be full."

Conclusion

Agape love is not a mere emotion but an action-oriented form of love that bears tangible fruits. These fruits are the litmus test of the authenticity of our love, serving both to edify the individual and build up the community in a manner that reflects the very character of God. Hence, it is no surprise that Paul emphasized that the greatest of the triad of faith, hope, and love is indeed love.

CHAPTER 9 Act in Harmony with Jesus' Loving Prayer

Jesus' Actions After Celebrating the Passover in 33 C.E.

In 33 C.E., after celebrating the Passover with His apostles, Jesus engaged in several profound actions and teachings, culminating in what is often referred to as His "High Priestly Prayer" in John 17. These actions set the stage for the events that would follow, leading to His crucifixion and ultimate glorification.

The Foot-Washing Ceremony

Before the Passover meal, Jesus washed the feet of His apostles, demonstrating the importance of humble service. He then instructed them to wash one another's feet, setting a model of humility and service that was foundational to Christian living (John 13:4-17).

The Institution of the Lord's Supper

Jesus took the bread and the wine during the meal and instituted the Lord's Supper or the Communion. He said the bread was His body, broken for them, and the wine was the new covenant in His blood (Matthew 26:26-28; Luke 22:19-20).

The Farewell Discourse

After the meal, Jesus delivered what is known as the "Farewell Discourse," recorded in John chapters 14-16. In this discourse, He assured His apostles of the coming of the Holy Spirit and emphasized the need for them to abide in Him as branches in the vine (John 15:1-5).

The Promise of Persecution and Divine Aid

He also warned them of impending persecution but assured them of the victory they would have in Him (John 16:33). These teachings were essential, equipping the apostles for the trials and tribulations they would face after His departure.

High Priestly Prayer

Finally, as recorded in John 17, Jesus offered a fervent prayer to His Father. Here He acknowledged that "the hour has come," signifying the approaching climax of His earthly ministry, which was His sacrificial death and subsequent resurrection. This prayer had a threefold focus:

1. **Jesus' Prayer for Himself**: He prayed for His glorification, so that in turn, He may glorify the Father (John 17:1-5).

2. **Jesus' Prayer for His Apostles**: He prayed for the spiritual safety of His apostles, whom He described as having been given to Him by the Father. He asked for their sanctification and unity (John 17:6-19).

3. **Jesus' Prayer for Future Believers**: Finally, He prayed for those who would come to faith through the apostolic message, that they might all be one, just as He and the Father are one (John 17:20-26).

The Significance of These Actions

Each of these actions, teachings, and prayers were aimed at preparing His apostles for the life and ministry that lay ahead of them. The foot-washing served as a lesson in humility, the Communion as a symbol of the New Covenant, the Farewell Discourse as a source of comfort and instruction, and the High Priestly Prayer as a final, solemn entrustment of His apostles—and indeed all future believers—to the protective and sanctifying care of the Father.

All of these elements point to a key theological principle: Jesus acted not only in awareness of the "hour" that had come but also in deep concern for the welfare and unity of His followers. He knew the challenges and tribulations they would face and, through these final actions and prayers, provided them with the necessary spiritual resources to endure and ultimately triumph.

The Big Change That Followed Jesus' Death

After Jesus' death on the cross, several monumental changes occurred that would forever alter the course of human history and the condition of mankind's relationship with God.

The Torn Veil

One of the most immediate and significant signs that something extraordinary had happened was the tearing of the temple veil from top to bottom at the moment of Jesus' death (Matthew 27:51). This act symbolized that the way into the Holy of Holies was now open for all, not just the High Priest. This marked the end of the old Levitical system and heralded the new covenant where every believer has direct access to God (Hebrews 10:19-22).

Resurrection and Ascension

Three days after His death, Jesus resurrected, providing irrefutable evidence that His sacrifice was acceptable to God and that death had been conquered (1 Corinthians 15:3-8, 20-22). Forty days after His resurrection, He ascended into heaven, signifying His exaltation and the commencement of His heavenly reign (Acts 1:9-11; Ephesians 1:20-23).

The Outpouring of the Holy Spirit

On the day of Pentecost, the Holy Spirit came upon the apostles, enabling them to speak in different languages and thereby launch the public proclamation of the gospel (Acts 2). This was in fulfillment of Jesus' promise and marked the birth of the Church.

The Spread of Christianity

The gospel message spread rapidly throughout the Roman Empire and beyond, resulting in the establishment of Christian communities that were rooted in the teachings of Jesus and the apostles (Acts; Romans 1:8).

Questions to Consider Regarding Jesus' Prayer in John 17

Given the background of these momentous changes that followed Jesus' death, one should consider several important questions regarding His prayer in John 17:

1. **How Did Jesus' Prayer for His Disciples' Unity Relate to the Changes That Followed His Death?** Jesus prayed for the unity of His followers (John 17:11, 21-23). How well are we contributing to that unity, especially considering the breaking down of divisions through the new covenant?

2. **What Does Sanctification Mean in the Context of Jesus' Prayer?** Jesus prayed for the sanctification of His disciples through the truth (John 17:17). How are we allowing the Word of God to sanctify us, in a world so filled with falsehoods?

3. **How Does Jesus' Prayer Illuminate His Role in God's Redemptive Plan?** In the prayer, Jesus speaks of the glory He had with the Father before the world began (John 17:5). What does this indicate about His divine nature and role in the redemptive plan of God?

4. **What Role Does Love Play in the Disciples' Relationship with God?** Jesus speaks of the love that the Father has for Him and extends this love to His disciples (John 17:24, 26). How does this love impact our understanding of God and our relationship with Him?

By thoroughly reflecting on these questions in light of Jesus' prayer, we can gain deeper insights into the profound theological and practical implications of His final moments before His arrest and subsequent death. These considerations, in turn, help us to align ourselves more closely with the will and purposes of God as revealed in the life, death, and resurrection of Jesus Christ.

The Introduction to Jesus' Prayer: Insights and Implications

The introduction to Jesus' prayer in John 17:1 reveals several profound aspects concerning Jesus' relationship with His Father, His awareness of the divine timetable, and His focus on God's glory.

Jesus' Relationship with the Father

The very act of lifting His eyes to heaven signifies a direct and intimate connection with the Father. Jesus does not resort to elaborate rituals or formalities; He speaks directly to His Father, indicating an existing relationship rooted in divine unity and mutual love.

Recognition of the Divine Timetable

When Jesus says, "the hour has come," He is acknowledging that the pivotal moment in God's redemptive plan has arrived. This suggests that Jesus was acutely aware of the divine timetable and willing to submit to it, regardless of the suffering He knew would ensue (Luke 22:42).

The Centrality of God's Glory

The dual request to "glorify your Son, that the Son may glorify you" indicates that the underlying motive for everything Jesus does is to bring glory to the Father. Even at this critical juncture, facing betrayal and crucifixion, Jesus' primary concern is the glorification of God.

How the Father Answered Jesus' Personal Request About His Future

The Father's response to Jesus' request for glorification is multifaceted, covering different phases of Jesus' work and exaltation.

The Crucifixion and Resurrection

Firstly, the Father answered Jesus by allowing Him to go through the crucifixion, the very means through which God's justice would be satisfied and humanity could be reconciled to God (Romans 3:24-26; Colossians 1:19-20). The subsequent resurrection of Jesus from the dead served as divine affirmation or vindication of His sacrifice (Romans 1:4; Acts 17:31).

The Ascension and Exaltation

Secondly, Jesus was exalted through His ascension into heaven, where He sat down at the right hand of God, a position of supreme honor and authority (Hebrews 1:3; Philippians 2:9-11).

The Ongoing Work Through the Church

Finally, the Father continues to glorify the Son through the work of the Church, which proclaims Jesus as the Savior of the world and the rightful Lord of all (Matthew 28:18-20; Ephesians 1:22-23).

Preconditions for the Apostles to Receive Eternal Life

Eternal life, as defined in Scripture, is an ongoing, quality relationship with God the Father and Jesus Christ His Son (John 17:3). Therefore, for the apostles to receive eternal life, they had to meet certain conditions.

Faith in Jesus as the Messiah

First and foremost, they had to put faith in Jesus Christ as the Son of God and the promised Messiah. Jesus Himself stated, "For God so loved the world, that he gave his only Son, that whoever believes in him should not perish but have eternal life" (John 3:16).

Obedience to God's Commandments

While faith is the foundational requirement, it is not a passive faith but one that leads to action. Jesus stated that if anyone loved Him, they would keep His commandments (John 14:15). This is in line with what is written elsewhere in the New Testament, that faith without works is dead (James 2:26).

Endurance Until the End

The apostles also needed to "endure to the end" to be saved (Matthew 24:13). They had to face various trials, persecutions, and even martyrdom but needed to remain steadfast in their faith.

Evidence That the Apostles Succeeded

We have multiple lines of evidence to suggest that the apostles did, in fact, fulfill these conditions for eternal life.

Witness of the New Testament

The New Testament itself bears witness to the apostles' faithfulness. For example, after Jesus' ascension, they were continually devoted to prayer and proclamation of the Word (Acts 1:14, 2:42). They faced persecution but rejoiced that they were counted worthy to suffer for the Name (Acts 5:41).

Their Writings

The epistles written by the apostles such as Peter, John, and Paul attest to their enduring faith and commitment to the teachings of Jesus Christ. Their writings are replete with encouragement for other believers to continue in the faith, which reflects their own adherence to the faith.

Martyrdom

Tradition and historical records indicate that most of the apostles faced martyrdom and chose to die rather than recant their faith in Jesus Christ. This ultimate sacrifice serves as a strong testament to their unwavering faith.

Jesus' Own Testimony

In John 17, within the prayer that serves as our foundational text, Jesus Himself prayed for His apostles, asking the Father to keep them in His name, sanctify them in the truth, and ultimately that they may be with Him to behold His glory (John 17:11, 17, 24). The very fact that Jesus interceded for them in such a manner implies a strong assurance of their faithfulness.

The Meaning of "Knowing" God

In the context of Scripture, "knowing" God goes far beyond mere intellectual acknowledgment of His existence or understanding His attributes. The concept carries with it a profound depth that involves a personal, intimate relationship with God. In the Hebrew Scriptures, the term "know" is sometimes used to describe the most intimate relations between a husband and a wife (Genesis 4:1). In a similar vein, knowing God means to have a deep, ongoing relationship with Him.

Experiential Knowledge

"Knowing" God in the biblical sense involves experiential knowledge. It is not merely a mental agreement with a set of doctrines or the acknowledgment of historical facts about Jesus Christ. It is a lived experience that transforms one's life. The Apostle Paul spoke of his own intimate knowledge of Christ when he said, "that I may know him and the power of his resurrection, and may share his sufferings, becoming like him in his death" (Philippians 3:10).

Covenantal Relationship

This "knowing" is often set in the context of a covenantal relationship. For instance, God said to Israel, "You only have I known of all the families of the earth" (Amos 3:2). This doesn't mean God was unaware of other nations, but rather that He had a special, covenantal relationship with Israel.

The Importance of Knowing God

The significance of knowing God cannot be overstated. Here are some reasons why it is critically important:

Eternal Life

Jesus Himself stated, "And this is eternal life, that they know you, the only true God, and Jesus Christ whom you have sent" (John 17:3). The attainment of eternal life is directly tied to knowing God and His Son.

Transformational Change

Knowing God leads to sanctification. The more one knows God, the more one becomes like Him (2 Corinthians 3:18). This is a transformational change that impacts all aspects of life.

Proper Worship

True worship stems from knowing God. Jesus said that the true worshipers will worship the Father in spirit and truth (John 4:23). Without knowing God, one's worship becomes empty ritual or mere emotionalism.

Assurance in Suffering

A deep and intimate knowledge of God provides assurance in times of suffering and trial. The Apostle Peter encouraged believers to rejoice in sufferings because it meant that they were sharing in Christ's sufferings and would thus know the glory to be revealed (1 Peter 4:13).

Effective Prayer

Knowing God also shapes our prayer life. In John 17, Jesus' prayer for His disciples is based on His intimate knowledge of the Father's will. The more we know God, the more aligned our prayers will be with His will.

Jesus' Primary Concern During His Earthly Ministry

Jesus' primary concern during His earthly ministry was to do the will of His Father in heaven and to glorify Him. The recurring themes in the Gospels underline Jesus' unwavering focus on fulfilling the Father's plan, which included the proclamation of the Kingdom of God, teaching God's laws, and ultimately, giving His life as a ransom for many (Matthew 20:28).

The Proclamation of the Kingdom

Jesus began His public ministry with the announcement of the Kingdom of God (Mark 1:15). This Kingdom is the realm where God's will is done, and it was central to Jesus' teaching.

Teaching and Healing

He not only proclaimed good news but also demonstrated the Kingdom's power through miracles, healing, and casting out demons. His teaching provided the ethical framework for living in accordance with the will of God (Matthew 5-7).

The Ultimate Sacrifice

The zenith of this focus on the Father's will was Jesus' sacrificial death on the cross. In the Garden of Gethsemane, He prayed, "not as I will, but as you will" (Matthew 26:39). His willingness to go to the cross was in perfect alignment with His primary concern—glorifying the Father.

Religious Traditions Jesus Would Have Rejected

Jesus would have rejected any religious traditions that subverted the Word of God and obstructed people from coming into a genuine relationship with the Father.

Hypocrisy and Legalism

He strongly condemned the Pharisees and scribes for their legalistic approach to God's laws and their hypocrisy.

He said, "They tie up heavy burdens, hard to bear, and lay them on people's shoulders, but they themselves are not willing to move them with their finger" (Matthew 23:4).

Traditions Over Commandments

Jesus criticized the religious leaders for nullifying God's commandments for the sake of their traditions. One classic example is when the Pharisees chastised Jesus' disciples for not washing their hands before eating, a tradition that had no basis in the Mosaic Law. Jesus countered by highlighting how the Pharisees themselves neglected the more important matters of the Law such as justice, mercy, and faithfulness (Matthew 15:1-9; 23:23).

Exclusivism and Elitism

Jesus also opposed the exclusionary practices of the religious elite who considered themselves the sole custodians of religious truth. He rebuked them for shutting the Kingdom of God in people's faces and for not entering themselves (Matthew 23:13).

Jesus Making Known His Father's Name

The act of Jesus making known His Father's name involves much more than simply telling people what to call God. It is a comprehensive revelation of the character, will, and purposes of God. In the Bible, a name often signifies the nature or attributes of the person bearing that name. Thus, when Jesus says he has made known the Father's name, he is referring to a full disclosure of who God is, what He is like, and what He intends to accomplish.

Revelation of God's Attributes

Jesus revealed the holiness, righteousness, love, and mercy of God in His teachings and actions. The Sermon on the Mount, for instance, lays out the moral and ethical standards of the Kingdom of God, reflective of God's character (Matthew 5–7).

Unveiling God's Salvific Will

Through His death and resurrection, Jesus clarified the Father's will to provide salvation for humanity. As Jesus noted, "For God so loved the world, that he gave his only Son, that whoever believes in him should not perish but have eternal life" (John 3:16).

Fulfilled Messianic Prophecies

By fulfilling Messianic prophecies, Jesus authenticated His role as the one sent by the Father and thus revealed God's predetermined plan. This had the effect of making known the Father's name, or rather, His nature and purposes (Luke 24:44–47).

The Goal for Jesus' Disciples

The overarching goal for Jesus' disciples should be to continue this work of making known the Father's name—that is, His character, will, and purposes—to the world.

Spreading the Gospel

The most direct way to achieve this is through the spreading of the Gospel. Before His ascension, Jesus gave the Great Commission: "Go therefore and make disciples of all nations, baptizing them in the name of the Father and of the Son and of the Holy Spirit, teaching them to observe all that I have commanded you" (Matthew 28:19-20).

Personal Sanctification

However, this work is not limited to words alone; it also includes personal sanctification. Living a life that reflects the character of God is a way to make His name known. "You are the salt of the earth...You are the light of the world" (Matthew 5:13–14).

Unity and Love Among Believers

The unity and love among believers also serve this goal. Jesus prayed for the unity of His disciples so that the world may believe that the Father sent Him (John 17:21). When disciples maintain unity and show love for one another, they affirm the truth that Jesus has made known the Father's name.

Persevering in Faith

Given the challenges and persecutions that Christians may face, persevering in faith is essential for this goal. This ties back to Jesus' High Priestly Prayer in John 17 where He prayed not just for His disciples but also for those who would believe through their word (John 17:20).

Necessities for Lifesaving Work: Insights from John 17:15-21

The High Priestly Prayer of Jesus in John 17 provides invaluable guidance for Christians involved in the work of saving lives spiritually. While Jesus covers various themes in this prayer, focusing on verses 15-21 reveals three critical elements necessary for succeeding in this lifesaving endeavor.

1. Divine Protection from the Evil One

John 17:15: "I do not ask that you take them out of the world, but that you keep them from the evil one."

Significance:

Jesus understood that Christians would remain in the world, exposed to both its allure and its threats. His prayer was not for isolation but for protection from the evil influences orchestrated by Satan, the Evil One. This protection is essential for anyone engaged in spiritual work, for one cannot help save others if one is endangered oneself.

Practical Application:

Christians should continuously seek divine protection through prayer and a life of godliness. Keeping oneself "unstained from the world" (James 1:27) is essential to remain effective in the mission.

2. Sanctification Through the Truth

John 17:17: "Sanctify them in the truth; your word is truth."

Significance:

Sanctification, or setting apart for a holy purpose, is a requirement for the lifesaving work Christians are to undertake. Jesus identifies the agent of this sanctification as "the truth," directly tying it to God's word. Being sanctified enables us to be holy representatives of God.

Practical Application:

Christians should dedicate themselves to the study of Scriptures, applying its principles in life, thereby setting themselves apart for divine service. The Apostle Paul urged Timothy to be a "worker...rightly handling the word of truth" (2 Timothy 2:15), which is advice that holds for all Christians.

3. Unity Among Believers

John 17:21: "that they may all be one, just as you, Father, are in me, and I in you, that they also may be in us, so that the world may believe that you have sent me."

Significance:

Jesus prays for unity among His followers similar to the unity that exists between Him and the Father. This unity is not merely a nice-to-have feature but a necessity for the world to recognize the divine origin and authority of Jesus' mission, and by extension, the mission of His followers.

Practical Application:

Believers must strive to maintain unity in the body of Christ, avoiding divisions, and schisms that could undermine the effectiveness of their lifesaving work. The Apostle Paul addresses this when he says, "I appeal to you, brothers, by the name of our Lord Jesus Christ, that all of you agree, and that there be no divisions among you, but that you be united in the same mind and the same judgment" (1 Corinthians 1:10).

Jesus' Prayer and Its First Century Fulfillment

The prayer Jesus offered in John 17 is one of the most profound in the New Testament, laying the groundwork for key doctrines and practices in the Christian faith. Let us look at how this prayer was answered during the first century C.E.

Glorification of the Son and the Father

John 17:1: "Father, the hour has come; glorify your Son, that the Son may glorify you."

Answered Through the Resurrection and Ascension:

The prayer for glorification finds its first fulfillment in the Resurrection. After Jesus' death, the power of God raised Him from the dead, thereby not only confirming His divinity but also glorifying Him (Romans 1:4; 6:4). This glory was further manifested when Jesus ascended to heaven and sat at the right hand of God (Mark 16:19; Hebrews 1:3).

Significance:

By resurrecting and exalting Jesus, the Father glorified the Son. The Son, in turn, used this glorified state to further bring glory to the Father by functioning as the Mediator and High Priest for mankind (1 Timothy 2:5; Hebrews 4:14). Therefore, Jesus' request for mutual glorification was indeed fulfilled.

Sanctification and Truth

John 17:17: "Sanctify them in the truth; your word is truth."

Answered Through the Apostolic Teachings:

Jesus' disciples were sanctified, set apart for holy use, through the truth as delivered by the Apostles (Ephesians 2:20; 2 Peter 1:16-21). The apostolic letters and teachings carried this sanctifying truth.

Significance:

The truth imparted through the Apostles was a means of sanctification for the early church. This sanctification was necessary for them to be effective witnesses and to carry out the divine mandate of discipleship (Matthew 28:19-20).

Unity Among Believers

John 17:21: "that they may all be one, just as you, Father, are in me, and I in you, that they also may be in us, so that the world may believe that you have sent me."

Answered Through the Formation of the Church:

The formation of the first-century Church bore evidence to the unity Jesus prayed for. Despite various backgrounds and ethnicities, believers displayed a remarkable sense of unity (Acts 2:44-47; 4:32).

Significance:

This unity served as a compelling testimony to the world, and indeed the church grew rapidly (Acts 6:7; 9:31). It supported the idea that the origin of this community was divine, thereby fulfilling Jesus' intention that the unity of believers would serve as a sign to the world of His messianic credentials.

The Unfulfilled Aspects of Jesus' Prayer Post-100 C.E.

While Jesus' prayer in John 17 was richly fulfilled in many aspects during the early church period, it is evident that certain aspects have not remained fulfilled after the apostolic age. This period, particularly after the death of the Apostle John around 100 C.E., saw a great deviation from the original teachings and unity that marked the early church.

The Rise of Apostasy and Division

Acts 20:29-30: "I know that after my departure fierce wolves will come in among you, not sparing the flock; and from among your own selves will arise men speaking twisted things, to draw away the disciples after them."

Historical Evidence of Division:

As mentioned by historians like Will Durant, the unity of the Church began to disintegrate rapidly after the Apostolic age. This was in line with what Paul warned about in Acts 20:29-30. The once-unified body of believers began to splinter into sects, some of which were at significant doctrinal odds with each other. By the second and fourth centuries, multiple heretical sects had arisen.

Significance:

The original unity and doctrinal purity Jesus prayed for had been compromised. This was not just a difference in minor doctrines but significant divergences that affected the core of Christian belief and practice.

A Multiplicity of Denominations Today

Current Reality:

Today, we see an even more fractured landscape with around 41,000 denominations. Even within a single denomination, like the Baptists, there are as many as 66 different sub-denominations. This splintering has led to a dilution of the gospel message and challenges in evangelism.

Significance:

Such division has made it nearly impossible to speak of a single "Christianity" but rather "Christianities" in the plural. This disunity is a stark deviation from the unity in truth Jesus prayed for in John 17.

Weak Evangelism and Lack of Growth

Statistics on Evangelism:

The statistics on evangelism are also telling. Only a minority of churchgoers actively engage in evangelistic efforts. Most new believers are born into Christian families, and very few conversions occur because of direct evangelism.

Significance:

This lack of evangelistic fervor signifies a broader spiritual malaise. It calls into question the extent to which modern believers are living out the Great Commission (Matthew 28:19-20), which was one of the tasks that the early church took seriously as a part of their sanctification and unity in truth.

Thus, after the apostolic age, particularly after the death of John around 100 C.E., the Church has seen a significant decline in maintaining the unity and sanctity that Jesus prayed for in John 17. Apostasy set in, divisions became rampant, and the fervor for evangelism has diminished significantly. This state of affairs underscores the need for a return to the original teachings and practices laid down in the New Testament to better align with Jesus' prayer and intentions for His followers.

The Path to Unity and Evangelism in Modern Times

The question of fulfilling Jesus' prayer for unity and evangelistic efficacy in a world of 41,000 Christian denominations is undeniably challenging. The disunity is not merely organizational but also doctrinal, often extending to salvation-level beliefs. However, difficult as the task might be, it's not impossible.

1. Revisiting Core Doctrines for Unity

Biblical Basis:

The foundation for unity has to be laid upon the "apostles' teaching" (Acts 2:42). All believers should strive for the unity of faith and knowledge of Jesus (Ephesians 4:13).

Possible Action:

Christians should return to the basics of the faith, focusing on the "elementary doctrines" (Hebrews 6:1-2), and reach a consensus on salvation-level issues.

Significance:

Until Christians can agree on these core beliefs, unity remains elusive. Churches should invest time in doctrinal study and debate with the aim of clarifying core beliefs and setting aside non-essential differences.

2. Empowering Lay Christians for Evangelism

Biblical Basis:

The Great Commission (Matthew 28:19-20) was not just given to a specific class of 'professional Christians' but to all believers.

Possible Action:

Churches need to train and empower their congregations for personal evangelism. Evangelistic programs must not be confined to sending out a few missionaries; the task is for all believers.

Significance:

By making evangelism a core part of every Christian's life, churches can begin to emulate the active evangelistic lifestyle of the early church.

3. Creating a Culture of Accountability

Biblical Basis:

The early Christians held each other accountable (James 5:16). The letters to the seven churches in Revelation (chapters 2-3) are also a testament to the necessity of continuous evaluation.

Possible Action:

To gauge the extent to which they are achieving unity and evangelistic effectiveness, churches should develop a culture of regular self-examination and accountability.

Significance:

Regular checks help ensure that churches stay true to their scriptural mission, thereby increasing the likelihood of fulfilling Jesus' prayer in modern times.

Can We Attain First Century Oneness Before Jesus Returns?

Luke 18:8: "When the Son of man comes, will He really find faith on the earth?"

Given the current scenario, achieving first-century unity seems like an uphill battle. However, Jesus' words in Luke 18:8 and Matthew 7:21-23 seem to indicate that the focus will be more on the individual's relationship with God and the "doing of God's will" rather than belonging to a particular denomination. Hence, while the ideal remains the attainment of unity, individuals should focus on personal sanctification and the propagation of core gospel truths.

Conclusion

While achieving complete unity may seem like an insurmountable task given the present scenario, Christians should strive for it by focusing on core doctrines, empowering all believers for evangelism, and establishing accountability mechanisms. Whether or not unity is fully achieved, individuals should seek to do the will of the Father, for it is those who do so who will be recognized when Christ returns (Matthew 7:21-23).

CHAPTER 10 What Does God Require of Us?

God's Requirements in Worship

The concept of God having requirements for those who seek to worship Him might raise questions in some minds. Why would an all-loving God set prerequisites? The Bible provides insights that help us understand the rationale behind God's requirements and why they are not only necessary but also beneficial for mankind.

1. God is Holy

Biblical Basis:

"You shall be holy, for I am holy" (1 Peter 1:16).

Explanation:

God's inherent nature is one of purity, righteousness, and holiness. Because of His holy nature, it is logical that there are standards and guidelines for approaching Him. Just as a ruler or monarch on Earth would have certain protocols for an audience, it stands to reason that the Supreme Ruler of the Universe would have standards for those approaching Him in worship.

2. Order and Consistency in God's Character

Biblical Basis:

"For God is not a God of disorder but of peace" (1 Corinthians 14:33).

Explanation:

Throughout the Scriptures, it is evident that God values order and consistency. The meticulous details provided in the construction of the Tabernacle, the precise laws given to Israel, and the prophetic timelines showcase God's nature of orderliness. Hence, it follows that the worship acceptable to such a God would have certain requirements to ensure order and consistency.

3. Protection and Well-being of Worshippers

Biblical Basis:

"I have the right to do anything," you say—but not everything is beneficial. "I have the right to do anything"—but not everything is constructive" (1 Corinthians 10:23).

Explanation:

God's requirements are never arbitrary. They are designed for the protection, well-being, and spiritual growth of His worshippers. By adhering to God's requirements, believers are shielded from harmful practices, ideologies, and behaviors that could jeopardize their spiritual and sometimes even physical well-being.

4. Genuine Love Manifested in Obedience

Biblical Basis:

"For this is the love of God, that we keep his commandments. And his commandments are not burdensome" (1 John 5:3).

Explanation:

God's requirements are a means by which believers can manifest their genuine love for Him. By adhering to these requirements, they show that their love is not mere lip service but is expressed through obedient actions. Moreover, God's commandments are not oppressive or overbearing; they are designed to be within reach of all who genuinely seek to obey them.

It is not surprising that a holy, orderly, and loving God has requirements for worship. These prerequisites are a reflection of His character and are designed for the benefit of His worshippers. Those who approach God with a genuine heart will find that His commandments, far from being burdensome, are a source of blessing, guidance, and protection.

Solomon's Summation of God's Expectations

Ecclesiastes 12:13 provides a profound yet succinct summation of human duty in relation to God. Solomon, known for his unparalleled wisdom granted by Jehovah, penned these words as the conclusion to his reflective and often contemplative book of Ecclesiastes.

The Context of Ecclesiastes

To understand the depth of Solomon's summation, it's important to consider the context of the entire book of Ecclesiastes. Throughout its chapters, Solomon explores various pursuits of life, from pleasure and wealth to wisdom and toil, often labeling them as "vanity" or "a striving after wind."

He analyzes life's cyclical nature and the inherent dissatisfaction found in many human endeavors. Yet, he also acknowledges the joy in life's simple pleasures and the importance of acknowledging God in youth before the "evil days" come.

Solomon's Summation

Biblical Basis:

"The end of the matter; all has been heard. Fear God and keep his commandments, for this is the whole duty of man" (Ecclesiastes 12:13).

Explanation:
After all his observations and reflections on life's complexities, Solomon distills his wisdom into a simple yet profound statement:

1. **Fear God**: This is not about being terrified of God but rather having a deep reverence, respect, and awe for Him. To fear God means recognizing His supreme authority, acknowledging His righteous standards, and being keenly aware of His ever-watchful eye.

2. **Keep His Commandments**: Obedience to God's commandments is the practical application of the fear of God. It's one thing to acknowledge God's greatness, but true reverence is demonstrated through obedience. As stated in **1 John 5:3**, loving God is intrinsically tied to keeping His commandments. Moreover, these commandments are not burdensome but are designed for our well-being and happiness.

The phrase, "for this is the whole duty of man," underscores the centrality of these two principles in human existence. All other pursuits, whether wealth, honor, pleasure, or wisdom, are secondary to this primary duty.

Relevance to Today's Believers

In a world filled with distractions and competing philosophies, Solomon's words serve as a compass for believers. While societal norms and values may change, the foundational duty of revering God and obeying His commandments remains constant. This is the path to true fulfillment, purpose, and eternal life.

Solomon, with his unmatched wisdom, identified the essence of human duty and purpose in relation to God. By fearing God and obeying His commandments, we not only fulfill our primary duty but also find meaning and purpose in an otherwise perplexing world.

Understanding the Greek Word "Burdensome"

Literal Meaning: βαρύς (barús)

The Greek word translated as "burdensome" in 1 John 5:3 is **βαρύς** (barús). At its most foundational level, this word means "heavy." In a literal sense, it can describe the weight of an object, indicating something that is physically heavy. However, in a figurative context, such as in 1 John 5:3, it can denote something that is hard to bear, challenging, or burdensome.

Why God's Commandments Are Not "Burdensome"

1. **Simplified Commandments in Christianity**: The teachings and instructions under the new covenant, brought forth by Jesus and the apostles, revolve predominantly around love—love for God

and love for our fellow humans. Jesus himself summarized all the commandments into two: loving God and loving our neighbor (Matthew 22:37-40). Such commandments, grounded in love, naturally align with our created purpose and, therefore, do not feel like an oppressive burden.

2. **Empowerment through the Holy Spirit**: While the commandments of God require Christians to live by high moral standards, believers are not left to fulfill these commands solely through their strength. Though we are not indwelt by the Holy Spirit, we are guided by the Spirit-inspired Word of God, which empowers and enlightens us in our journey of faith.

3. **Comparison with Pharisaic Laws**: Many first-century Jews were bogged down by the extensive Mosaic Law, which was compounded by the additional traditions and interpretations added by the Pharisees. Jesus criticized the Pharisees for binding heavy burdens on the people (Matthew 23:4). In contrast, the commandments emphasized by Jesus and the apostles were more straightforward, focusing on the heart rather than mere ritualistic observances.

4. **The Motive Behind the Commandments**: God's commandments are designed for our well-being. They are not arbitrary rules but are given out of love and are meant for our benefit. When one understands that these commandments reflect God's love and wisdom, it becomes easier to view them not as burdens but as guidelines for a meaningful and fulfilling life.

5. **Positive Outcomes**: Following God's commandments leads to genuine happiness, a clean conscience, and a life that is pleasing to our Creator. The positive outcomes of living in harmony with God's standards further affirm that they are not burdensome but beneficial.

While the word βαρύς points to something being heavy or hard to bear, the context of 1 John 5:3 emphasizes that God's commandments, when understood and followed in the light of love and divine guidance, are not oppressive. Instead, they are a source of joy, peace, and genuine freedom.

Dependency of Our Salvation

Foundation of Salvation: Knowing God and Jesus Christ

In John chapter 17, particularly in verse 3, Jesus provides profound insight into the foundation of salvation. He says:

"This is eternal life, that they may know You, the only true God, and Jesus Christ whom You have sent." (John 17:3, UASV)

From this, several foundational truths become clear:

1. **Knowledge of God and Jesus**: Salvation isn't merely about a superficial acknowledgment of God and Jesus Christ. It's about *knowing* them intimately. This knowledge isn't merely intellectual; it's relational. It's a knowledge borne out of a close relationship, like the bond between close friends or family.

2. **Belief in the "Only True God"**: This implies that there are false representations and understandings

of God. Salvation is dependent on recognizing and knowing the *true* God—the God of the Scriptures.

3. **Recognizing Jesus' Role**: It's not just about knowing God but also recognizing and accepting Jesus Christ as the one sent by God. This encompasses understanding Jesus' role in God's salvation plan, his teachings, his sacrifice, and his position as the mediator between God and humanity.

Obedience to God's Commands

Building on the foundation laid in John 17:3, 1 John 5:3 emphasizes that love for God is manifested in *keeping His commandments*. Thus, genuine knowledge of and relationship with God and Jesus will naturally lead to obedience. This obedience isn't viewed as burdensome but is carried out with joy and love.

"For this is the love of God, that we keep his commandments. And his commandments are not burdensome," (1 John 5:3, UASV)

The Unity of Believers

Further in John chapter 17, Jesus prays for the unity of his followers (John 17:20-21). This unity isn't merely organizational but is based on shared beliefs, values, and purpose. Such unity is likened to the unity between the Father and the Son. Being part of this united group, the Christian congregation, is vital for salvation.

Being Sanctified by Truth

Jesus prays, *"Sanctify them in the truth; your word is truth."* (John 17:17, UASV). To be sanctified means to be set apart for a holy purpose. The instrument for this sanctification is the truth—God's Word. Therefore, our salvation is also dependent on our relationship with God's Word, our acceptance of it, and our living in harmony with its truths.

In essence, our salvation, as highlighted in John chapter 17 and supported by 1 John 5:3, is dependent on:

- An intimate knowledge of and relationship with the only true God and Jesus Christ.

- Loving obedience to God's commandments.

- Being a part of the united body of true believers.

- Living in harmony with the truths of God's Word, allowing it to sanctify our lives.

Salvation isn't based on mere ritualistic practices or superficial faith but on a profound, intimate relationship with God and Jesus, manifesting itself in obedient love and unity with fellow believers.

Taking in Knowledge' of God in Greek

The Greek Understanding

To fully understand the phrase 'taking in knowledge' of God, we must delve into the Greek text of the New Testament, specifically the verb used in passages that emphasize knowing God.

The primary verb in the Greek New Testament that translates as "to know" is γινώσκω (ginōskō). This verb has a range of meanings, but within the context of knowing God, it refers to a deep, experiential knowledge, not just an intellectual or superficial awareness.

Beyond Mere Intellect

The Greek understanding of *ginōskō* in relation to knowing God is not merely an accumulation of facts or doctrines. Instead, it conveys:

- **Intimate Acquaintance**: Just as one might know a close friend or family member.

- **Experiential Knowledge**: It's a knowledge born out of experience, a relational understanding that grows over time.

- **Recognizing and Acknowledging**: It's more than just being aware; it's a full recognition and acknowledgment, often leading to transformative action.

In John 17:3, Jesus said, *"This is eternal life, that they may know (ginōskō) You, the only true God, and Jesus Christ whom You have sent."* The use of *ginōskō* here underscores a profound, relational, and experiential knowledge of God and Jesus Christ, which is central to obtaining eternal life.

Relation to Love and Obedience

As highlighted in the foundational text, the genuine knowledge of God is closely tied to love and obedience. *1 John 5:3* states, *"For this is the love of God, that we keep his commandments. And his commandments are not burdensome."* This suggests that truly knowing God— in the *ginōskō* sense— will inevitably lead to loving obedience to His commandments.

To 'take in knowledge' of God in the Greek understanding is to develop a deep, experiential, and relational knowledge of Him. It's not a passive or purely intellectual endeavor. Instead, it's an active, ongoing relationship marked by love, obedience, and transformative growth. This knowledge is the foundation for eternal life and the genuine worship of the only true God.

Learning About God Through Creation

Nature's Testimony of God's Existence

"The heavens declare the glory of God; the skies proclaim the work of his hands." (Psalm 19:1, UASV). This verse and many like it throughout the Scriptures emphasize the belief that the natural world is a testament to the existence and qualities of its Creator. Here are specific aspects of creation that can teach us about God:

1. God's Immense Power

The sheer magnitude and vastness of the universe, with its billions of galaxies and even more stars, reveal a Creator of incomprehensible power. The very existence of the universe and the finely-tuned laws of physics that govern it suggest a purposeful and potent force behind everything. *"Lift up your eyes to the heavens, and look at the earth beneath; for the heavens will vanish like smoke, the earth will wear out like a garment." (Isaiah 51:6, UASV).*

2. God's Artistry and Appreciation for Beauty

From the intricate patterns found in the smallest snowflake to the breathtaking views of a sunset over a mountain range, the beauty in creation points to a Designer with an appreciation for beauty and aesthetics. This shows that God not only made things to be functional but also to be enjoyed, reflecting His own sense of beauty.

3. God's Wisdom and Precision

The precision in the way the natural world operates, from the cellular processes in our bodies to the way the planets orbit in our solar system, speaks to a Creator with infinite wisdom and understanding. The ecological balance, the water cycle, the photosynthesis process, and countless other examples in nature exhibit an intricately designed system that works with precision.

4. God's Sustenance and Provision

Creation reveals a God who is not distant but is actively involved in sustaining and providing for His creation. Whether it's the way rainfall nourishes the land or the complex ecosystem where every organism has a role to play, it speaks of a Provider who cares for His creation. *"He covers the heavens with clouds; he prepares rain for the earth; he makes grass grow on the hills." (Psalm 147:8, UASV)*

5. God's Love for Diversity

The immense variety in creation, from the numerous species of animals to the different landscapes around the world, reflects a Creator who appreciates diversity and uniqueness. This can teach us about God's inclusive love for all and His appreciation for individuality.

Looking at creation gives us a glimpse of God's character and His attributes. While nature alone cannot give us a complete picture of God – that requires a personal relationship and understanding of the Scriptures – it certainly serves as a starting point, drawing mankind's attention to the existence of a powerful, wise, and loving Creator. As Romans 1:20 (UASV) says, *"For his invisible attributes, namely, his eternal power and divine nature, have been clearly perceived, ever since the creation of the world, in the things that have been made."* This means that through creation, humanity is without excuse in acknowledging God.

Taking in Knowledge of God: A Joy, Not a Burden

1. The Innate Human Desire to Know the Creator

Humans have an intrinsic yearning to understand their purpose and to know their Creator. This is evident in the religious history of humanity and the spiritual quests many undertake. By taking in knowledge of God and His purposes, this innate desire is satisfied, offering clarity and purpose to our existence. The Psalmist expressed this innate desire when he said, *"As a deer pants for flowing streams, so pants my soul for you, O God." (Psalm 42:1, UASV)*.

2. The Joy of Discovering God's Love

The deeper one delves into understanding God, the clearer His love becomes. Recognizing that the Creator of the universe cares for each individual is a profound and uplifting realization. The love God has shown – especially through the sacrifice of His Son – is a testament to His care and concern for humanity. *"By this the love of God was manifested in us, that God has sent His only begotten Son into the world so that we might live through Him." (1 John 4:9, UASV)*. Understanding this love naturally creates a reciprocative love in us for God, making the act of learning about Him a joy rather than a burden.

3. God's Commandments Promote True Well-being

The laws and principles set out in Scripture are not arbitrary rules but are designed for our well-being. When we understand and apply them, we often experience better physical, mental, and emotional health. This makes God's commandments appealing and beneficial. *"Happy is the man who finds wisdom and the man who gains understanding." (Proverbs*

3:13, UASV). God's guidelines, when understood correctly, are not onerous but are, in fact, the path to a fulfilling and meaningful life.

4. Knowledge Leads to Freedom

Jesus himself said, *"You will know the truth, and the truth will set you free." (John 8:32, UASV).* The knowledge of God and His purposes liberates us from misconceptions, superstitious fears, and the burdensome traditions of men. With a clear understanding of God's will, one is freed from the uncertainty and confusion that often plague those searching for spiritual direction.

5. Strengthened Relationship with God

The more we know someone, the deeper our relationship with that person can become. The same holds true with God. Taking in knowledge of Him and His purposes allows for a closer, more personal relationship with the Creator. Through this relationship, believers often find strength, comfort, and guidance in their daily lives.

While some might view religious practices and study as burdensome, taking in knowledge of God is far from a tiresome obligation. It is a fulfilling journey that brings clarity, purpose, and joy. Just as John wrote, God's commandments, which include the command to take in knowledge of Him, are not burdensome. They are a manifestation of His love and a guide to a truly enriching life.

Making Changes in Accordance with the Knowledge of God

1. Cultivating a Christlike Attitude

As we deepen our understanding of God, we ought to emulate the qualities and attributes of Jesus Christ, who is the perfect reflection of His Father. *"Whoever says he abides in him ought to walk in the same way in which he walked." (1 John 2:6, UASV).* This includes developing qualities like love, patience, kindness, humility, and forgiveness.

2. Prioritizing Spiritual Matters

With an increased knowledge of God, our values and priorities should shift towards spiritual matters. *"But seek first the kingdom of God and his righteousness, and all these things will be added to you." (Matthew 6:33, UASV).* Activities such as prayer, Bible study, and Christian fellowship should become central in our lives.

3. Demonstrating Love Towards Others

The knowledge of God is intrinsically linked to the love of God. As we grow in understanding, our love for God and for our neighbors should also grow. *"We love because he first loved us." (1 John 4:19, UASV).* This love is manifest in our actions, words, and attitudes towards others.

Avoiding Unclean Practices

The Bible highlights various unclean practices that those seeking to please God should avoid:

- **Sexual Immorality:** Fornication, adultery, and other forms of sexual misconduct are explicitly condemned. *"Flee from sexual immorality."* *(1 Corinthians 6:18, UASV).*

- **Idolatry:** This includes not only the worship of physical idols but also placing undue importance on anything above God, such as money, status, or other material pursuits. *"Therefore, my beloved, flee from idolatry."* *(1 Corinthians 10:14, UASV).*

- **Lying and Deception:** Speaking the truth is a fundamental principle in the life of a Christian. *"Therefore, having put away falsehood, let each one of you speak the truth with his neighbor."* *(Ephesians 4:25, UASV).*

- **Substance Abuse:** Overindulgence in alcohol or the use of drugs can impair judgment and lead one away from God. *"Do not get drunk with wine, for that is debauchery."* *(Ephesians 5:18, UASV).*

- **Unholy Associations:** Associating with individuals or groups that promote values or practices contrary to God's standards can be spiritually harmful. *"Do not be deceived: 'Bad company ruins good morals.'"* *(1 Corinthians 15:33, UASV).*

Taking in the knowledge of God is not merely an intellectual pursuit but a transformative one. It requires changes in thought, attitude, and action. By adhering to God's commandments and refraining from unclean practices, believers demonstrate their genuine love for God and their desire to walk in His ways. Such a path, while requiring effort and sacrifice, is neither burdensome nor tedious but is the route to a life filled with purpose, joy, and the hope of eternal blessings.

God's Requirements: Actions and Beliefs

God's requirements for His worshipers encompass both their beliefs and their behavior. These two domains—what we believe and how we act—intertwine and inform one another, manifesting a genuine relationship with God.

1. Treatment of Others

- **Love as a Fundamental Command:** One of the foremost commandments from God is that we should love our neighbors as ourselves. *"You shall love your neighbor as yourself." (Matthew 22:39, UASV).* This love should reflect in our actions, words, and decisions.

- **Forgiveness:** Jesus emphasized the need for forgiveness, implying that if we expect God to forgive us, we too must forgive others. *"And whenever you stand praying, forgive, if you have anything against anyone, so that your Father also who is in heaven may forgive you your trespasses." (Mark 11:25, UASV).*

- **Justice and Equity:** God commands that we act justly and fairly with others, highlighting the importance of honesty and equity in our dealings. *"You shall do no injustice in judgment, in measures of length or weight or quantity." (Leviticus 19:35, UASV).*

2. What We Believe

- **Acknowledging Jesus as the Christ:** Our salvation is tied to our belief in Jesus as the Messiah, the Son of God. *"Whoever believes that Jesus is the Christ is born of God." (1 John 5:1, UASV).*

- **Resurrection:** A cornerstone of Christian belief is in the resurrection of Jesus. This belief is vital to our hope and faith. *"If you confess with your mouth that Jesus is Lord and believe in your heart that God raised him from the dead, you will be saved." (Romans 10:9, UASV)*.

- **Belief in God's Word:** A believer is expected to accept the Bible as the inspired Word of God. *"All Scripture is inspired by God and profitable for teaching, for reproof, for correction, for training in righteousness." (2 Timothy 3:16, UASV)*.

Beliefs Informing Actions

The beliefs we hold shape our actions. For instance, if we truly believe in Jesus' teachings on love and forgiveness, it will manifest in our behavior. Similarly, understanding and believing that every human is made in the image of God *(Genesis 1:27, UASV)* would naturally lead us to treat others with respect and dignity.

Actions Reflecting Beliefs

Conversely, our actions can also serve as a testament to our beliefs. James reminds us that faith without works is dead *(James 2:26, UASV)*. This indicates that genuine belief in God's commandments should produce corresponding actions.

God's requirements seamlessly blend beliefs with behavior. By keeping His commandments, believers not only demonstrate their love for God but also validate their beliefs through actions. Such a holistic approach to worship ensures that faith is not merely an intellectual or emotional endeavor but is rooted in real-life practice, mirroring the holistic nature of God's love described in *1 John 5:3*: love that is true, active, and uncompromising.

God's Standards: A Joy, Not a Burden

The Scripture makes it clear that God's commandments are designed for our benefit, and adhering to them should not be viewed as burdensome. By examining the nature of God, the purpose behind His commandments, and the outcome of following them, we can gain a deeper understanding of why it is not a burden to measure up to God's standards for right conduct and to accept His truth.

1. The Loving Nature of God

- **God as Our Creator:** God, as our Creator, knows our design, needs, and what is truly beneficial for us. His standards and truths are therefore aligned with our best interests. *"For I know the plans I have for you, declares Jehovah, plans for welfare and not for evil, to give you a future and a hope." (Jeremiah 29:11, UASV).*

- **Expression of Love:** God's commandments are an expression of His profound love for us. As *1 John 5:3* puts it, adhering to His commandments is a reflection of our love for Him, and these commandments are not burdensome. They are meant for our good, to protect, guide, and bless us.

2. The Purpose Behind God's Commandments

- **Protection:** Many of God's standards safeguard us from harm. For instance, prohibitions against lying, stealing, or committing adultery serve to protect our relationships, our integrity, and our well-being.

- **Moral and Ethical Living:** God's commandments provide a framework for moral and ethical living, which ensures a harmonious and just society. *"You shall love your neighbor as yourself: Love does no wrong to a neighbor; therefore love is the fulfilling of the law." (Romans 13:9-10, UASV).*

- **True Freedom:** By following God's standards, we experience true freedom. Not the freedom to act on every impulse, but the freedom from the consequences of harmful actions. *"The truth will set you free." (John 8:32, UASV).*

3. The Outcome of Following God's Standards

- **Inner Peace:** Those who follow God's standards often find an inner peace knowing they are walking in alignment with their Creator's will. *"And the peace of God, which surpasses all understanding, will guard your hearts and your minds in Christ Jesus." (Philippians 4:7, UASV).*

- **Blessings:** Adherence to God's standards often leads to blessings, both tangible and intangible. *"If you walk in my statutes and observe my commandments and do them, then I will give you your rains in their season, and the land shall yield its increase, and the trees of the field shall yield their fruit." (Leviticus 26:3-4, UASV).*

- **Eternal Prospects:** Aligning ourselves with God's standards has eternal implications, leading to everlasting life. *"And this is eternal life, that they know you, the only true God, and Jesus Christ whom you have sent." (John 17:3, UASV).*

God's standards for right conduct and His truths are designed with our best interests at heart. They are not arbitrary rules but are rooted in His immense love and deep understanding of our needs. When we recognize the love behind the commandments and the benefits of adhering to them, it becomes clear that they are not burdensome.

Instead, they pave the way for a fulfilling, joyous, and purposeful life both now and eternally.

Identifying True Christians: A Glimpse into First-Century Christianity

The early Christians in the first century C.E. left a profound blueprint for their faith and practices, which can serve as a benchmark to identify authentic Christianity today. Let us delve into the Scriptures and historical context to discern the determining marks of true Christians, echoing the foundation laid by first-century believers.

1. Love for One Another

- **The Hallmark of Christianity:** Jesus himself declared, *"By this all people will know that you are my disciples, if you have love for one another." (John 13:35, UASV).* Love was not merely an emotion but an action, where believers looked out for each other's interests, even to the point of laying down their lives for their brethren.

- **Selfless Acts:** They sold their properties and belongings to support fellow believers in need (Acts 2:44-45, UASV).

2. Adherence to Apostolic Teaching

- **Solid Foundation:** True Christians remained steadfast in the apostles' teaching and were not swayed by every wind of doctrine (Acts 2:42, UASV).

- **Guarding Against Apostasy:** They were constantly on guard against false teachings and apostasy (Acts 20:29-30, UASV).

3. Evangelistic Zeal

- **Spreading the Good News:** Early Christians took the Great Commission seriously, making disciples throughout their known world (Matthew 28:19-20, UASV).

- **Facing Persecutions:** Their evangelistic efforts often brought persecution, but they rejoiced in sharing in Christ's sufferings (Acts 5:41, UASV).

4. Keeping God's Commandments

- **Obedience from the Heart:** As *1 John 5:3* points out, their love for God was manifested in their obedience to His commandments. They understood that God's commandments were not burdensome but a reflection of His love and wisdom.

5. Participating in Congregational Worship and Fellowship

- **Meeting Together:** They regularly met together for prayer, breaking of bread, and studying the Scriptures, strengthening the bonds of brotherhood (Acts 2:46-47, UASV).

6. Living Morally Upright Lives

- **Separate from the World:** They were in the world but not of it, maintaining high moral standards and not conforming to the surrounding pagan cultures (Romans 12:2, UASV).

- **Fleeing from Immorality:** Sexual immorality, dishonesty, and other vices were shunned (1 Corinthians 6:18-20, UASV).

7. Recognizing the Role of Jesus Christ

- **Central to Faith:** Jesus Christ was at the core of their faith. They recognized his sacrificial role, his resurrection, and his position as the mediator between God and man (1 Timothy 2:5, UASV).

8. Led by the Spirit Inspired Word of God

- **Guided by Scriptures:** Their beliefs and practices were rooted in the Scriptures. They did not rely on mere traditions or human philosophies but were guided by the Spirit-inspired Word of God.

In the maze of religious beliefs and practices prevalent today, the above marks, grounded in first-century Christianity, provide a clear template to identify true Christians and authentic Christianity. As believers strive to emulate these benchmarks, they come closer to the genuine faith practiced by the early followers of Jesus Christ.

Obligation Towards Those in the World: Guided by 1 Timothy 2:3-4

The world around us is often depicted in the Scriptures as a tumultuous sea, filled with challenges, temptations, and wickedness. As Christians, we are called to be a beacon of light, shining amidst the darkness. But what exactly is our duty towards those who are yet to find their way out of this "wicked world"? The Apostle Paul offers profound insight into this matter in his letter to Timothy.

God's Desires and Our Obligation

The text in *1 Timothy 2:3-4* reads: "This is good, and it is acceptable in the sight of God our Savior, who desires all people to be saved and to come to the knowledge of the truth." (UASV)

From this passage, we glean the following responsibilities:

1. Desire for All to be Saved

- **God's Heart:** Our God, who is full of compassion and mercy, desires that all should come to salvation. His wish is not for any to perish but for all to attain eternal life (2 Peter 3:9, UASV).

- **Our Role:** As God's representatives on earth, it is our obligation to align our desires with His, longing for the salvation of everyone, even those who may oppose or persecute us.

2. Promote the Knowledge of Truth

- **Truth as the Anchor:** The pathway to salvation is not just through faith but through a genuine understanding and acceptance of the truth of God's Word.

- **Our Responsibility:** As Christians, it is incumbent upon us to not only live by the truth but also to share the truth with others. This involves teaching, preaching, and making disciples, fulfilling the Great Commission (Matthew 28:19-20, UASV).

3. Demonstrating Genuine Christian Love

- **Not Burdensome:** As emphasized in *1 John 5:3*, our adherence to God's commandments, which includes loving our neighbor, is not burdensome. It's a manifestation of our love for God.

- **Evangelistic Zeal:** Our love for God and humanity should motivate us to reach out to those "in the waters of this wicked world," offering them hope, truth, and the chance for salvation.

4. Persistent Prayer

- **Intercessory Prayer:** Earlier in the same chapter of Timothy, Paul encourages believers to offer prayers and intercessions for all people (1 Timothy 2:1, UASV). This means continually praying for the spiritual awakening of those in the world.

In essence, our obligation to those still navigating the treacherous waters of this world is vast yet profoundly simple: to mirror God's love and desire for all to come to salvation and the knowledge of truth. This is accomplished through our words, actions, prayers, and our unyielding commitment to sharing the Gospel message with all.

Bibliography

Akin, Daniel L. *The New American Commentary: 1, 2, 3 John.* Nashville, TN: Broadman & Holman , 2001.

Akin, Daniel L., David P. Nelson, and Jr. Peter R. Schemm. *A Theology for the Church.* Nashville: B & H Publishing, 2007.

Alden, Robert L. *Job, The New American Commentary, vol. 11 .* Nashville: Broadman & Holman Publishers, 2001.

Alleman, H. C., and E. E. Flack. *Old Testament Commentary.* Philadelphia: Fortress Press, 1954.

Anders, Max. *Holman New Testament Commentary: vol. 8, Galatians-Colossians .* Nashville, TN: Broadman & Holman Publishers, 1999.

—. *Holman Old Testament Commentary - Proverbs .* Nashville: B&H Publishing, 2005.

Anders, Max, and Doug McIntosh. *Holman Old Testament Commentary - Deuteronomy (pp. 359-360). .* Nashville: B&H Publishing, 2009.

Anders, Max, and Trent Butler. *Holman Old Testament Commentary: Isaiah.* Nashiville, TN: B&H Publishing, 2002.

Andrews, Edward D. *AN INTRODUCTION TO BIBLE DIFFICULTIES So-Called Errors and Contradictions.* Cambridge: Christian Publishing House, 2011.

—. *An Introduction to Bible Difficulties: So-called Errors and Contradictions.* Cambridge, OH: Christian Publlishing House, 2012.

—. *BIBLE DIFFICULTIES: Debunking the Documentary Hypothesis.* Cambridge: Christian Publishing House, 2011.

—. *BOOKS OF 2 JOHN 3 JOHN and JUDE CPH New Testament Commentary.* Cambridge: Christian Publishing House, 2013.

Archer, Gleason L. *A Survey of Old Testament Introduction.* Chicago: Moody, 1994.

—. *Encyclopedia of Bible Difficulties.* Grand Rapids: Zondervan, 1982.

Arnold, Clinton E. *Zondervan Illustrated Bible Backgrounds Commentary Volume 2: John, Acts. .* Grand Rapids, MI: Zondervan, 2002.

—. *Zondervan Illustrated Bible Backgrounds Commentary Volume 3: Romans to Philemon.* Grand Rapids: Zondervan, 2002.

—. *Zondervan Illustrated Bible Backgrounds Commentary Volume 4: Hebrews to Revelation.* Grand Rapids, MI: Zondervan, 2002.

—. *Zondervan Illustrated Bible Backgrounds Commentary: Matthew, Mark, Luke, vol. 1.* Grand Rapids, MI: Zondervan, 2002.

Balz, Horst, and Gerhard Schneider. *Exegetical Dictionary of the New Testament.* Edinburgh: T & T Clark Ltd, 1978.

Barker, Kenneth L., and Waylon Bailey. *The New American Commentary: vol. 20, Micah, Nahum,*

Habakkuk, Zephaniah. Nashville, TN: Broadman & Holman Publishers, 2001.

Bercot, David W. *A Dictionary of Early Christian Beliefs.* Peabody: Hendrickson, 1998.

Blomberg, Craig. *The New American Commentary: Matthew .* Nashville, TN : Broadman & Holman Publishers, 2001.

—. *The New American Commentary: Matthew.* Nashville, TN: Broadman & Holman Publishers, 1992.

Boa, Kenneth, and Kruidenier. *Holman New Testament Commentary: Romans.* Nashville: Broadman & Holman, 2000.

Boa, Kenneth, and William Kruidenier. *Holman New Testament Commentary: Romans.* Nashville: Broadman & Holman, 2000.

Boles, Kenneth L. *The College Press NIV commentary: Galatians & Ephesians.* Joplin, MO: College Press, 1993.

Borchert, Gerald L. *The New American Commentary: John 1-11 .* Nashville, TN: Broadman & Holman Publishers, 2001.

Borchert, Gerald L. *The New American Commentary vol. 25B, John 12–21.* Nashville: Broadman & Holman Publishers, 2002.

Boyd, Gregory A, and Paul R Eddy. *Across the Spectrum [Secon Edition].* Grand Rapids: Baker Academic, 2002, 2009.

Brand, Chad, Charles Draper, and England Archie. *Holman Illustrated Bible Dictionary: Revised, Updated and Expanded.* Nashville, TN: Holman, 2003.

Bratcher, Robert G., and Howard Hatton. *A Handbook on the Revelation to John.* New York: United Bible Societies, 1993.

Bromiley, Geoffrey W. *The International Standard Bible Encyclopedia (Vol. 1-4).* Grand Rapids, MI: William B. Eerdmans Publishing Co., 1986.

Bromiley, Geoffrey W., and Gerhard Friedrich. *Theological Dictionary of the New Testament, ed. Gerhard Kittel, vol. 4.* Grand Rapids, MI: Eerdmans, 1964-.

Brotzman, Ellis R. *Old Testament Textual Criticism.* Grand Rapids: Baker Academic, 1994.

Bullinger, Ethelbert William. *Figures of Speech Used in the Bible.* London; New York: E. & J. B. Young & Co., 1898.

Buter, Trent C. *Holman New Testament Commentary: Luke.* Nashville, TN: Broadman & Holman Publishers, 2000.

Butler, Trent C. *Holman New Testament Commentary: Luke.* Nashville, TN: Broadman & Holman Publishers, 2000.

Calloway, Brent A. *THE BOOK OF JAMES: CPH CHRISTIAN LIVING COMMENTARY.* Cambridge: Chriwstian Publishing House, 2015.

Collins, John. *Genesis 1-4: A Linguistic, Literary, and Theological Commentary.* Philipsburg: P&R, 2006.

Cooper, Lamar Eugene. *The New American Commentary, Ezekiel, vol. 17.* Nashville, TN: Broadman & Holman Publishers, 1994.

Cooper, Rodney. *Holman New Testament Commentary: Mark.* Nashville: Broadman & Holman Publishers, 2000.

Cornwall, Judson, and Stelman Smith. *The Exhaustive Dictionary of Bible Names.* Gainsville: Bridge-Logos, 1998.

Davis, Christopher A. *THE COLLEGE PRESS NIV COMMENTARY: Revelation.* Joplin: College Press Publishing Co., 2000.

Davis, John J. *Paradise to Prison: Studies in Genesis.* Salem: Sheffield, 1975.

Easley, Kendell H. *Holman New Testament Commentary, vol. 12, Revelation.* (Nashville, TN: Broadman & Holman Publishers, 1998.

Elliott, Charles. *Delineation Of Roman Catholicism: Drawn From The Authentic And Acknowledged Standards Of the Church Of Rome, Volume II.* New York: George Lane, 1941.

Elwell, Walter A. *Baker Encyclopedia of the Bible.* Grand Rapids: Baker Book House, 1988.

—. *Evangelical Dictionary of Theology (Second Edition).* Grand Rapids: Baker Academic, 2001.

Elwell, Walter A, and Philip Wesley Comfort. *Tyndale Bible Dictionary.* Wheaton, Ill: Tyndale House Publishers, 2001.

Enns, Paul P. *The Moody Handbook of Theology.* Chicago: Moody Press, 1997.

Erickson, Millard J. "Biblical Inerrancy: the last twenty-five years." *Journal of the Evangelical Theological Society,* 1982: 387-394.

—. *Introducing Christian Doctrine.* Grand Rapids: Baker Book House, 1992.

Erickson, Millard J. *The Concise Dictionary of Christian Theology.* Wheaton: Crossway Books, 2001.

Erickson, Milliard J. *Christian Theology (Third Edition).* Grand Rapids, MI: Baker Academic, 2013.

—. *Christian Theology.* Grand Rapids, MI: Baker Academic, 1998.

Ferguson, Everett. *Baptism in the Early Church: History, Theology, and Liturgy in the First Five Centuries .* Grand Rapids, MI: Eerdmans, 2009.

Friberg, Timothy, Barbara Friberg, and Neva F. Miller. *Analytical Lexicon of the Greek New Testament.* Grand Rapids: Baker Books, 2000.

—. *Analytical Lexicon of the Greek New Testament, Baker's Greek New Testament Library.* Grand Rapids, MI: Baker Books, 2000.

Friedman, Richard Elliot. *Who Wrote The Bible.* San Francisco: Harper Collins, 1997.

Friedman, Richard Elliott. *The Bible With Sources Revealed.* Northampton: Harper Collins, 2005.

Gangel, Kenneth O. *Holman New Testament Commentary: Acts.* Nashville, TN: Broadman & Holman Publishers, 1998.

Gangel, Kenneth O. *Holman New Testament Commentary, vol. 4, John .* Nashville, TN: Broadman & Holman Publishers, 2000.

—. *Holman Old Testament Commentary: Daniel.* Nashville: Broadman & Holman Publishers, 2001.

Garland, David E. *1 Corinthians, Baker Exegetical Commentary on the New Testament.* Grand Rapids, MI: : Baker Academic, 2003.

Garrett, Duane. *Rethinking Genesis: The Sources and Authorship of the First Book of the Pentateuch .* Grand Rapids: Baker Books, 1991.

Geisler, Norman L. *Systematic Theology in One Volume.* Minneapolis, MN: Bethany House, 2011.

Geisler, Norman L., and Thomas Howe. *The Big Book of Bible Difficulties.* Grand Rapids: Baker Books, 1992.

George, Timothy. *The New American Commentary: Galatians .* Nashville, TN: Broadman & Holman Publishers, 2001.

Green, Joel B, Scot McKnight, and Howard Marshall. *Dictionary of Jesus and the Gospels.* Downers Grove, IL: InterVarsity Press, 1992.

Grudem, Wayne. *Making Sense of the Bible: One of Seven Parts from Grudem's Systematic Theology (Making Sense of Series).* Grand Rapids: Zondervan, 2011.

Gruden, Wayne. *Are Miraculous Gifts for Today?: 4 Views (Counterpoints: Bible and Theology).* Grand Rapids: Zondervan, 2011.

Gunkel, Hermann. *The Stories of Genesis. Translated by John J. Scullion. Edited by William R. Scott.* Berkeley: BIBAL, 1994.

Harris, Robert Laird, Gleason Leonard Archer, and Bruce K Waltke. *Theological Wordbook of the Old Testament.* Chicago: Moody Press, 1999, c1980.

Harrison, R. K. *Introduction to the Old Testament.* Massachusetts: Hendrickson, 2004.

Hastings, James, John A Selbie, and John C Lambert. *A Dictionary of Christ and the Gospels.* New York, NY: Charles Scribner's Sons, 1907.

Hill, Jonathan. *Zondervan Handbook to the History of Christianity.* Oxford: Lion, 2006.

Hindson, Ed, and Ergun Caner. *The Popular Encyclopedia of Apologetics: Surveying the Evidence for the Truth of Christianity.* Eugene: Harvest House, 2008.

Hoerth, Alfred. *Archaeology and the Old Testament.* Grand Rapids: Baker, 1998.

Holmes, Michael W. *The Apostolic Fathers: Greek Texts and English Translations.* Grand Rapids: Baker Academics, 2007.

House, Paul R., and Eric Mitchell. *Old Testament Survey (2nd Edition).* Nashville, TN: B&H Publishing Group, 2007.

Kaiser Jr., Walter C. *The Old Testament Documents: Are They Reliable & Relevant?* Downer Groves: InterVarsity Press, 2001.

Kass, Leon R. *The Beginning of Wisdom: Reading Genesis.* New York: Free Press, 2003.

Keener, Craig S. *The IVP Bible Background Commentary: New Testament.* Downer Groves, IL: InterVarsity Press, 1993.

Keil, Carl Friedrich, and Franz Delitzsch. *Commentary on the Old Testament.* Peabody, MA: Hendrickson, 1996.

Kenneth, Boa., and Kruidenier. *Holman New Testament Commentary: Romans, Vol. 6.* Nashville, TN: Broadman & Holman, 2000.

Kissling, Paul J. *The College Press NIV commentary: Genesis.* Joplin, MO: College Press Pub. Co., 2004.

Kitchen, K A. *On the Reliability of the Old Testament.* Grand Rapids: Eerdmans, 2003.

—. *The Ancient Orient and the Old Testament.* Chicago: Tyndale Press, 1966.

Kitchen, K. A. *Ancient Orient and Old Testament.* Downers Grove, IL: InterVarsity Press, 1975.

Kittel, Gerhard, Gerhard Friedrich, and Geoffrey William Bromiley. *Theological Dictionary of the New Testament.* Grand Rapids: Eerdmans, 1995, c1985.

Knight, George W. *The Layman's Bible Handbook.* Uhrichsville: Barbour Publishing, 2003.

—. *The Pastoral Epistles: A Commentary on the Greek Text, New International Greek Testament Commentary.* Grand Rapids, MI; Carlisle, England: W.B. Eerdmans; Paternoster Press, 1992.

Koehler, Ludwig. "Problem in the Study in the Language of the Old Testament." *Journal of Semitic Studies,* 1956: 3-24.

Koehler, Ludwig, Walter Baumgartner, M E J Richardson, and Johann Jakob Stamm. *The Hebrew and Aramaic Lexicon of the Old Testament.* Leiden; New York: E. J. Brill, 1999.

Lange, J. P. *Commentary of the Holy Scriptures: Revelation.* New York: Scribner's, 1872.

Language, John Peter. *A Commentary on the Holy Scriptures: Genesis.* Bellingham: Logos Research Systems, 1939, 2008.

Larson, Knute. *Holman New Testament Commentary, vol. 9, I & II Thessalonians, I & II Timothy, Titus, Philemon.* Nashville, TN: Broadman & Holman Publishers, 2000.

Lasor, William Sanford, David Allan Hubbard, and Frederic Williams Bush. *The Message, Form, and Background of the Old Testament: Old Testament Survey (2nd ed.).* Grand Rapids: Wm. B. Eerdmans, 1996.

Lea, Thomas D. *Holman New Testament Commentary: Vol. 10, Hebrews, James.* Nashville, TN: Broadman & Holman Publishers, 1999.

Lea, Thomas D., and Hayne P. Griffin. *The New American Commentary, vol. 34, 1, 2 Timothy, Titus.* Nashville: Broadman & Holman Publishers, 1992.

Longman III, Tremper. *How to Read Genesis.* Downers Groves, IL: Intervarsity Press, 2005.

Longman, Tremper III, and Raymond B Dillard. *An Introduction to the Old Testament.* Grand Rapids: Zondervan, 2006.

Martin, D Michael. *The New American Commentary 33 1, 2 Thessalonians .* Nashville, TN: Broadman & Holman, 2001, c1995 .

Mathews, K. A. *The New American Commentary vol. 1A, Genesis 1-11:26 .* Nashville: Broadman & Holman Publishers, 2001.

Matthews, K. A. *The New American Commentary Vol. 1B, Genesis 11:27-50:26.* Nashville: Broadman and Holman Publishers, 2001.

McMinn, Mark R. *Psychology, Theology, and Spirituality in Christian Counseling (AACC Library).* Carol Stream, IL: Tyndale House Publishers, 2010.

McReynolds, Paul R. *Word Study: Greek-English.* Carol Stream: Tyndale House Publishers, 1999.

Melick, Richard R. *The New American Commentary: vol. 32, Philippians, Colissians, Philemon.* Nashville, TN : Broadman & Holman Publishers, 2001.

Mirriam-Webster, Inc. *Mirriam-Webster's Collegiate Dictionary. Eleventh Edition.* Springfield: Mirriam-Webster, Inc., 2003.

Morris, Henry M. *The Genesis Record: A Scientific and Devotional Commentary on the Book of the Beginnings.* Grand Rapids: Baker Books, 2007, 1976.

Morris, Leon. *Tyndale New Testament Commentaries: Revelation.* Grand Rapids: William Eerdmans Publishing Company, 1987.

Mounce, Robert. *Robert Mounce, The New International Commentary of the New Testament: The Book of Revelation.* Grand Rapids: William Eerdmans Publishing Company, 1977.

Mounce, William D. *Mounce's Complete Expository Dictionary of Old & New Testament Words.* Grand Rapids, MI: Zondervan, 2006.

Mounce, William D. *Basics of Biblical Greek Grammar.* Grand Rapids: Zonervan, 2009.

Myers, Allen C. *The Eerdmans Bible Dictionary* . Grand Rapids, Mich: Eerdmans, 1987.

Osborne, Grant R. *BAKER EXEGETICAL COMMENTARY ON THE NEW TESTAMET: REVELATION.* Grand Rapids, MI: Baker Academic, 2002.

Oswalt, John N. *The NIV Application Commentary: Isaiah.* Grand Rapids, MI: Zondervan, 2003.

Polhill, John B. *The New American Commentary 26: Acts.* Nashville: Broadman & Holman Publishers, 2001.

Pratt Jr, Richard L. *Holman New Testament Commentary: I & II Corinthians, vol. 7.* Nashville: Broadman & Holman Publishers, 2000.

Pratt Jr, Richard L. *I & II Corinthians, vol. 7, Holman New Testament Commentary* . Nashville, TN: , 2000: Broadman & Holman Publishers, 2000.

Ramsey, Boniface (Editor). *Manichean Debate (Works of Saint Augustine).* New City Press: Hyde Park, 2006.

Reyburn, William David, and Euan Mc G. Fry. *A Handbook on Genesis (UBS Handbook Series).* New York: United Bible Societies, 1997.

Roberts, Alexander, James Donaldson, and A. Cleveland Coxe. *THE ANTE-NICENE FATHERS 1: The Apostolic Fathers with Justin Martyr and Irenaeus.* Buffalo: The Christian Literature Company, 1885.

Robertson, Paul E. "Theology of the Healthy Church." *The Theological Educator: A Journal of Theology and Ministry,* Spring 1998: 45-52.

Robinson, G. L., and R. K. Harrison. *The International Standard Bible Encyclopedia, vol. 2.* Grand Rapids: Eerdmans, 1982.

Ryken, Leland. *The Word of God in English.* Wheaton: Crossway Books, 2002.

Schaeffer, Francis A. *Genesis in Space and Time: The Flow of Biblical History.* Downers Groves: Intervarsity Press, 1972.

Smith, Gary. *The New American Commentary: Isaiah 1-39, Vol. 15a.* Nashville, TN: B & H Publishing Group, 2007.

—. *The New American Commentary: Isaiah 40-66, Vol. 15b.* Nashville, TN: B&H Publishing, 2009.

Speiser, E. A. *Genesis Anchor Bible 1.* Garden City: Doubleday, 1964.

Stein, Robert H. *A Basic Guide to Interpreting the Bible: Playing by the Rules.* Grand Rapids: Baker Books, 1994.

—. *The New American Commentary: Luke.* Nashville, TN: Broadman & Holman , 2001, c1992.

Swanson, James. *A Dictionary of Biblical Languages - Greek.* Washington: Logos Research Systems, 1997.

Swindoll, Charles R, and Roy B. Zuck. *Understanding Christian Theology.* Nashville, TN: Thomas Nelson Publishers, 2003.

Terry, Milton S. *Biblical Hermeneutics: A Treatise on the Interpretation of the Old and New Testaments.* Grand Rapids: Zondervan, 1883.

Thomas, Robert L. *New American Standard Hebrew-Aramaic and Greek Dictionaries: Updated Edition.* Anaheim: Foundation Publications, Inc., 1998, 1981.

—. *Revelation 1-7: An Exegetical Commentary* . Chicago, IL: Moody Publishers, 1992.

—. *Revelation 8-22: An Exegetical Commentary* . Chicago, IL: Moody Publishers, 1995.

Torrey, Reuben A., and Edward D. Andrews. *DIFFICULTIES IN THE BIBLE Alleged Errors and Contradictions: Updated and Expanded Edition.* Cambridge: Christian Publishing House, 2012.

Towns, Elmer L. *Concise Bible Dictries: Clear, Simple, and Easy-to-Understand Explanations of Bible Doctrines.* Chattanooga: AMG Publishers, 2006.

—. *Theology for Today.* Belmont: Wadsworth Group, 2002.

Vincent, Marvin. *Word Studies in the New Testament.* Bellingham: Logos Research Systems, 2002.

Vine, W E. *Vine's Expository Dictionary of Old and New Testament Words.* Nashville: Thomas Nelson, 1996.

Walls, David, and Max Anders. *Holman New Testament Commentary: I & II Peter, I, II & III John, Jude.* Nashville: Broadman & Holman Publishers, 1996.

Walton, John H. *Zondervan Illustrated Bible Backgrounds Commentary (Old Testament) Volume 1: Genesis, Exodus, Leviticus, Numbers, Deuteronomy.* Grand Rapids, MI: Zondervan, 2009.

—. *Ancient Near Eastern Thought and the Old Testament.* Grand Rapids: Baker Academic, 2006.

—. *Zondervan Illustrated Bible Backgrounds Commentary (Old Testament) Volume 3: 1 & 2 Kings, 1 & 2 Chronicles, Ezra, Nehemiah, Esthe.* Grand Rapids, MI: Zondervan, 2009.

—. *Zondervan Illustrated Bible Backgrounds Commentary (Old Testament) Volume 5: The Minor Prophets, Job, Psalms, Proverbs, Ecclesiastes, Song of Songs.* Grand Rapids, M: Zondervan, 2009.

Walton, John H. *THE NIV APPLICATION COMMENTARY Genesis.* Grand Rapids: Zondervan, 2001.

Walton, John H., Victor H. Matthews, and Mark W Chavalas. *The IVP Bible Background Commentary: Old Testament.* Downers Grove: IVP Academic, 2000.

Walvoord, John F. *Daniel: The Key to Prophetic Revelation.* Chicago, IL: Moody Publishers, 1971, reprint 1989.

Walvoord, John. *The Revelation of Jesus Christ.* Chicago: Moody Press, 1996.

Watson, Richard. *A Biblical and Theological Dictionary: Explanatory of the History, Manners and Customs of the Jews.* New York: Waugh and T. Mason, 1832.

Weatherly, Jon A. *THE COLLEGE PRESS NIV COMMENTARY: 1 & 2 Thessalonians.* Joplin: College Press Publishing Company, 1996.

Weber, Stuart K. *Holman New Testament Commentary, vol. 1, Matthew.* Nashville, TN: Broadman & Holman Publishers, 2000.

Whiston, William. *The Works of Josephus.* Peabody, MA: Hendrickson, 1987.

Wood, D R W. *New Bible Dictionary (Third Edition).* Downers Grove: InterVarsity Press, 1996.

Wuest, Kenneth S. *Wuest's Word Studies from the Greek New Testament: For the English Reader.* Grand Rapids: Eerdmans, 1997, c1984.

Zodhiates, Spiros. *The Complete Word Study Dictionary: New Testament.* Chattanooga: AMG Publishers, 2000, c1992, c1993.

Zuck, Roy B. *Basic Bible Interpretation: A Prafctical Guide to Discovering Biblical Truth.* Colorado Springs: David C. Cook, 1991.

www.ingramcontent.com/pod-product-compliance
Lightning Source LLC
LaVergne TN
LVHW041155080426
835511LV00006B/607